THE BOSS

THE BOSS

GLEN BOSS

MACMILLAN
Pan Macmillan Australia

This book is dedicated to Sloane, Tayte and Carter

First published 2007 in Macmillan by Pan Macmillan Australia Pty Limited
1 Market Street, Sydney

National Library of Australia
Cataloguing-in-Publication data:

Boss, Glen.
The Boss.

ISBN 9781405038195 (pbk.).

1. Boss, Glen. 2. Melbourne Cup (Horse race). 3. Jockeys –
Australia – Biography. 4. Makybe Diva (Race horse).
5. Horse racing accidents – China – Macau (Special
Administrative Region). I. Title.

798.40092

Typeset in 12 pt Sabon by Midland Typesetters, Australia
Printed in Australia by McPherson's Printing Group

Papers used by Pan Macmillan Australia Pty Ltd are natural, recyclable
products made from wood grown in sustainable forests. The manufacturing
processes conform to the environmental regulations of the country of origin.

Contents

Foreword

The Hon. John Brown, AO

Horse racing is a universal sport conducted with varying degrees of decorum. Nowhere in the world has it been as colourful, down-to-earth and demonstrative as in Australia. Fine horses and skilful riders have enjoyed a special respect since this country's earliest days, and the Melbourne Cup is without doubt a manifestation of Australia's love of racing. 'The race that stops a nation' is a truism emulated nowhere else in the world. The Australian Jockey Club has to grudgingly admit that in Sydney it is its biggest day of the year, attracting its largest on-course attendance; the federal parliament ceases its deliberation; and the betting turnover is a national phenomenon.

Every jockey's ambition is to win a Melbourne Cup. To retire after a distinguished career without a Cup win leaves a sad void in any rider's record. To win three successive Melbourne Cups would be any jockey's dream; to win three Cups on the same magnificent mare is a sublime achievement. That Glen Boss managed this astounding feat is legendary. Hall-of-fame trainer

Lee Freedman said '[Boss's] rides in the Melbourne Cup should be bottled up and studied. They have been perfect rides.'

In my experience of racing, there is no greater big-race rider than Glen Boss. When he gets in 'The Zone', his rides are invariably nerveless and astute. Sure, there are jockeys with better general statistics; sure, a lot of jockeys ride more winners on an annual basis. But when the Group 1 races come along – the ones that really count – there is no more consistently successful jockey than Glen. The figures tell the story. He has ridden more Group 1 winners from 2004 to 2006 than any other rider – 29 in total.

A top jockey is a superb and courageous athlete. Astride 600 kilograms of racehorse on a tiny piece of pigskin and travelling at 40 kilometres per hour is not a place for a wimp. Too many jockeys have lost their lives in the pursuit of winners; too many have become physically disabled as a result of racing accidents. Like any other jockey, Glen has taken the risks and suffered the consequences. In June 2002 Glen's career almost came to an end in a horrendous fall in Macau. Life in a wheelchair might well have been the result. However, the prompt action of a team of surgeons in Hong Kong, as well as Glen's great courage and resilience, allowed him to resume his career after only a few months in a halo brace.

Glen Boss is a remarkable young man – a jockey of peerless ability with a reputation for honesty and hard work. I know Glen very well and have the highest regard for his decency. The spectre of that fall in Macau has led him to sponsor a wheel-chair athlete through a foundation I run, and Glen is now back riding in Hong Kong, where his skills will enable him to reach the top in that most competitive arena. Think of great big-race jockeys – think of Glen Boss.

Prologue

The old car picks its way through the potholes until the elderly woman at the wheel spots a space by the fence near the final turn into the straight.

The boy, 15 and respectful enough to keep his mouth shut, remains broodingly unimpressed by the idea of his grandmother conscripting him to the adult world of the Gympie races. His body language can't hide the impression that he would rather be somewhere else.

With that studied indolence peculiar to the young, he steps squinting into the bright light of race day and the din of the public address system blaring out the progress of the runners in the first.

You can live a whole life – birth, play, work, death – and no single event comes along to yank you away from the ordinary existence destiny has lined up for you. It's not like it offered any clues, but on this day destiny is about to deal the boy a different hand.

Nothing in his young life could have prepared him for what happens next. He is standing by the fence, one hand resting on top of the car door in the motion of slamming it shut, when the field arrives at the turn. Mouth open like a farm gate, the boy is riveted by the most fantastic spectacle. Barely 30 metres away, banking into the turn like a river in monsoon flood, comes a heaving, roaring, muscular herd of horseflesh; brutal and beautiful, a wild thing seemingly beyond control, awesome in its power, daubed with the brilliant colours of the riders' silks and giving off a clamour of shouts and curses spliced with the snap of leather on hide. And, underneath it all, the utterly unforgettable anthem that would become the soundtrack for his very existence: the rolling thunder of thoroughbreds in full flight. Time seems to warp and stretch but it is probably little more than a moment and they are gone, a blur of tails, rumps and steel shoes, down the short straight.

His whole world turns. It is addiction at first sight.

1

The boy from the bush

Almost from the jump, it had been family, land and horses. I was born in Beaudesert on 21 August 1969, the second child of Terry and Lorraine Finglas. In short time, the young couple had produced four kids – Samantha, me, Kelly and baby Tina – three girls and a boy. We lived on a sizeable cattle property outside town while our father travelled into Beaudesert each day to work at his parents' cement business.

Lorraine Muggeridge's family hailed from the tough mining town of Mount Morgan and whatever dreams she had entertained as a bride evaporated when her marriage to Terry failed. I was about four when Mum packed us up and moved to Gympie, where she had relatives. I never saw or heard from Terry Finglas again.

You can't pass judgement on somebody you don't know which is why I have no particular image or opinion of my natural father. But, as a parent, I can appreciate how hard it must have been for Mum to go it alone with four kids in tow.

Before we settled into a tiny house in Gympie, we were welcomed by our relatives, the Rowlands family. They offered much more than refuge and kindness. At the front door of their home was a welcome mat. At the back, a vast paddock on which horses picked at the grass and greeted the arrival of strangers with alert eye and pricked ears. The Rowlands were horse people. The love of horses and their role in country life was a part of the family heritage. With my tiny paw in the reassuring grip of an adult, I was led out into this paddock to make the acquaintance of these majestic animals, stroke the extended muzzles as their mighty heads dipped to greet the newcomer. I was never afraid. Entranced, but never afraid.

The Rowlands knew an old bushie, a retired stockman, who lived on a nearby property. He was the genuine item, the sort of bloke who could have ridden with Clancy of the Overflow. He taught me to ride, legging me up bareback for the very first time, a diminutive four-year-old up on the back of a massive Clydesdale. A pebble on a mountain. To that time, I had been used to adults being in control of the world's big things – cars, machinery, keys that opened doors. The notion that this mighty horse, with a back so broad that my tiny legs were almost obliged to perform the splits, would respond to my feeble urgings was an incredible revelation to a small boy. Under the wise guidance of that old bushie, riding horses seemed so simple. My memory is of picking the skills up very quickly – balance, coordination, command, touch – almost without having to think about them.

All my early riding was done bareback. All you needed was a bridle and a good sense of balance. It came so natural to me and allowed such perfect communication between rider and horse that adapting to a saddle seemed like a backward step. Packing a large slab of leather between my bum and the horse hardly made any sense at all. If you were going to compete at pony club you needed the right gear, but when I first acquired a saddle, I didn't know what to do with it.

The move to Gympie was fortuitous in many ways. I learned to ride, competed at Gympie Pony Club on a painted horse called Pride, and Mum met a good man. His name was Tom Boss and he would become our dad, mentor and breadwinner. Traditionally, even a very young bull will resent an older bull moving into his territory. For a while, as young as I was, I had been the man in the family, the only male among four females. But with me and Tom, this was never the case. He was young, had no kids of his own and could have been excused for thinking twice about taking on a single mum with a ready-made brood. But, like everything Tom Boss tackled in life, he gave it his best shot. And that was more than good enough for me.

In the early '70s, the new family set up house on a small holding outside Caboolture. It was a mixed farm, mainly cattle and pigs. About 50 kilometres to the north of Brisbane, Caboolture is wedged between the surfing beaches of Bribie Island to the east and the rural expanses of Kilcoy to the west. North lies the Sunshine Coast. It was originally the home of the Kabi people who gave it the name 'Caboolture', meaning 'Place of the Carpet Snake'. The first white settlers started farming the area from 1841 and by the 1860s timber-getters were making real inroads on the precious red cedar, which they floated down the Caboolture River to Deception Bay from where it was shipped to Brisbane. In the 1970s, before the development boom really took hold of south-east Queensland and long before Caboolture became a place for show acreages from where business executives would commute daily to the office, it was what city folks would call 'the sticks' – pure country.

Life was busy and grew busier still when Mum brought baby Bob home from hospital, followed shortly by another little sister christened Leanne. The new arrivals meant Tom and Lorraine had six kids under their roof but nobody paused long enough to wonder how the parents could ever fend for such a mob. We were all too busy getting on with life itself. Besides the farm, Tom drew income from his contracting work as a slasher. He would always be first out of bed, jumping up into the tractor seat to head off before sun-up to slash a neighbour's paddock. In later years, as Caboolture's farms began to disappear under the advance of the residential boom, he would take a job as a quarry manager to supplement the family income. I never considered what we did to be hard work. It was just the stuff of life and I took it on like a second skin, rising in the pre-dawn light to do the chores of feeding and watering the animals, mucking out and cleaning up. Then, it was back inside to dress for school, wolf down breakfast and head off with my siblings to catch the school bus into Caboolture. As the eldest boy, when I was not at school I worked alongside Tom. He worked hard without complaint. That was the way. He taught me that work was its own reward and, when he saw that I could assume responsibility, allowed me to keep the proceeds from the sale of piglets I had weaned and reared from one of our breeding sows. It was my first entrepreneurial project and it generated some handy pocket money and an early sense of self-reliance. In years to come, that appetite for work, rising early and the discipline of tending animals would provide an ideal pattern for my professional life.

The farming life doesn't grant you too many days off, let alone paid annual leave. But, as a leisure outlet, Caboolture Pony Club seemed a good fit. Each Sunday we would be off to the local showground or a nearby town to compete, but not before shampooing the horses, plaiting their manes and tails and having them looking their best. It became a ritual that Mum laid out our gear on the Saturday night in readiness for an early start the next morning. When the program took us to another town like Redcliffe or Pine Rivers, the club horse truck would turn up, load our ponies and we would follow in the family car. We competed in age groups, entering about eight events on the day including flags, barrel racing, show jumping and dressage. Pride, the painted pony who had been my first ever horse, hadn't accompany us from Gympie to Caboolture as I had outgrown her. She was carted off for a comfortable life on a property owned by Tom's mum, another horse fancier who had embraced us all as her very own grandkids.

The tradition of hand-me-downs sustains large families and it was no exception at our place. The best hand-me-down I received from my elder sister Samantha was Sinbad. He was about eight years old, stood 13 to 14 hands high and was a fiery chestnut spiced with a bit of quarter horse and a dash of Arab. We were a great partnership and won ribbons galore.

It was Sinbad who taught me that some horses can go a whole lot quicker than others. The slow disciplines like dressage had their place, but I gravitated to the faster events. The partnership of two strong wills working in tandem to find that balance between flat-strap and perfect control was intoxicating. One by-product of going fast was the odd spill, but there was no fall severe enough to prevent me from jumping straight back on the horse. Speed was my thing and I lived for the thrill of going as fast as possible in cross-country jumping events.

My other sporting love helped with my pain threshold. Pony club occupied my weekends but for school sport in winter, rugby league was the only game in town, at least as far as I was concerned. It didn't matter that I was smallish for my age and got absolutely smashed by the bigger kids as I thrived on the physical contest, playing close to the action in the hooker position. The traffic in the middle of the ruck is always heaviest and, more often than not, I'd come off a very distant second from the one-on-one encounters. But all that changed with one telling tackle. An opposing player made a break and I was the only defender who could possibly run him down. Don't ask me where it came from, but every bit of timing and every molecule of muscle was packed into that one instant as I connected with the best hit of my fledgling footy career. The ball-carrier went down as if he'd been slammed by a cannonball. The bloke I tackled was surprised and so were my team-mates. But not as surprised as me. Later, the lesson would become obvious: You can be as big and strong as a bull but without timing, you've got nothing. From that point on, I prided myself on my defensive technique and made a point of letting nobody run past or through me. I was a tackling machine. The coach rewarded my new-found skill by converting me to fullback where he thought my deadly tackling would provide an unassailable last line of defence for Caboolture State High.

Whether tangling with bigger blokes or tumbling off horses, bumps and bruises were a constant part of my adolescence, each lump and purple patch a down-payment for what lay ahead.

It's in the bloodlines. To my mum, with her slight frame, goes the credit for the smallish build which defined my ultimate career choice. Halfway through high school, I had no thoughts of riding horses for a living. Rugby league was fun and so was long-distance running. The small chassis came with a big motor and I loved testing it out in school cross-country events. It seemed to come naturally to me as I never trained. Working around the farm, I was always in a hurry to get from one place to the next and would do it at a clip run, never at a walk. So when it came to tearing along barefoot with a pack of kids, I found that I had a natural appetite for the longer distances. The further we went, the more kids slowed or dropped out until there was only me out front, loping along at a comfortable pace. Coming up to a big race, it occurred to me that I should do a bit of training so I set off around our farm and other adjoining properties, which had a combined perimeter of about 10 kilometres. Two sessions seemed enough. The skinny, bare-foot kid from Caboolture kept running all the way to the State championships in Brisbane where he managed a third-placing against a field of older boys.

Between hard work, hard play and school, family life was harmonious. You might imagine six kids under the one roof would create bedlam, but we rarely blued. Samantha, the eldest, was a shining light, possessed with great nurturing instincts and a certain serenity that influenced us all. Today, she still lives in the area and, not surprisingly, has a large family of her own. As kids, we made our own fun and spent every waking hour outside in the fresh air. I'd get so engrossed in a project that even when Mum would call us for dinner, I'd be reluctant to tear myself away until it was completed. From an early age I had a commitment to doing things properly. It was a trait that would stick with me throughout life. Today, I am at a loss as to why people don't give their best in every endeavour. We weren't the richest kids in the district but we never really went without. As a family we gave each other all the right stuff. Our lives were full and we virtually fell exhausted into bed each night.

I couldn't have imagined how this life was preparing me so precisely for what lay ahead. Part of the pony club education involved equine theory where we learned all about the anatomy of a horse, its bone structure and how it worked, plus how horses behaved. We were regularly tested and I prided myself on getting pretty much all of it right. At school I was no great shakes, especially in subjects that bored me, but if I was interested and engaged the lessons hit their mark.

Without being big-headed about it, I knew I was a good rider simply by the amount of events I won. We had instructors at pony club but my improvement was largely due to trial and error, a process of finding out for myself what worked for me. Caboolture might have been a little off the beaten track but, when it came to learning about horses, we didn't miss a trick. One year, the pony club hosted an international coach and his wife from Germany. I nodded in approval when they mentioned the value of learning to ride bareback as an aid for developing balance.

When the trophy cabinet and ribbon box were full to overflowing I knew that the pony club had just about tested my limits. Boredom set in. It was about this time, in my mid teens, that I started educating horses, not for money but more for the challenge. While I was teaching horses, it slowly dawned that they were educating me. I'd be schooling them in the most rudimentary way how to jump by stepping over a log, or how to do the barrels. But, at the same time I was learning that all horses are different, are good at different things and learn in different ways. Some had sensitive mouths and required careful treatment; others would be bolters and you'd have to win their trust enough to teach them not to take flight at the slightest pretext. Tapping a horse's potential was a matter of getting inside its head. In a funny way, that's what I do today – help make an animal do its best.

It was a challenge. In the beginning I'd take on a horse that would have absolutely no idea. In or month or so it could perform competently as a jumper or a barrel racer. Back then, I didn't see it as a mental puzzle, but that's exactly what it was: the process of trying to fathom how an individual horse thinks. If one way wouldn't work, I'd try another until a pathway for communication identified itself. Then we had an understanding and could slowly build from that point. Horses are just like us: some pick their training up quickly and others require it over and over again before the lesson sinks in. For no apparent reason, one horse will be a good jumper but useless at anything else. You have to identify what works for them. Thinking back now, I can't really recall a method or a routine. Perhaps there wasn't one. I just did it.

Anybody who knows anything about making a horse go fast understands that you have to ride short, which means shortening the stirrups until your boots are tucked right up near the saddle. It positions your weight forward, which is the ideal balance point for riding at speed. I always rode short, standing up over the horse in my quest for pace. This trait didn't go unnoticed. One day, an old bloke who lived outside Caboolture on a spread where he trained quarter horses asked if I would be interested in helping exercise his string of horses. I'll never forget the first time on one of his speed machines. I started at one end of Caboolture Showground and this thing took off like the proverbial bat out of hell. In a blink, I was at the other end of the showground going whoo-hoo. I'd never been on anything that quick in my life, at least not without a motor. The acceleration was amazing! The rush, unbelievable!

At that time, in my mid teens, flat-chat was the thrill. Maybe it was my male hormones kicking in but the need for speed became like a drug. When I couldn't get it from riding quarter horses, I'd be throwing a leg over a dirt bike. Wearing nothing but a pair of rubber thongs, shorts and a helmet, me and my mates would hammer the living daylights out of our two-stroke off-roaders, wringing the throttle so hard it felt like the cylinder was about to blast through the head. I had two speeds: stop and flat out. There were spills galore and plenty of lost skin. But, at 15, you're inclined to believe you're bulletproof.

All this might have taken a predictable direction. I was bored with pony club, attracted to motor bikes and in a year or two I'd have my car licence. Chances are, like so many country blokes with too much time and testosterone, I'd be off burning rubber in a souped-up ute and roaring off at weekends to drink too much Bundaberg rum and raise a bit of hell. It just might have turned out that way but for the fact that during a holiday at my grandparents' place in Gympie my grandmother needed some company one particular day at the races.

2

Forget it, mate – you're too bloody big!

Call it love at first sight or addiction at first bite. Whatever it was, I was hooked. My grandmother didn't have to ask if I wanted to attend the next race meeting with her – she had been there for my conversion and had witnessed my rapture.

Tom Boss's mum was a bit of a fixture at Gympie gallops and knew the right people. It must have been on our return visit that she arranged a tour of the jockeys' room. As a kid who fancied himself as a horseman, an invitation to the inner sanctum was an unbelievable honour. From bush tracks to Flemington, the jockeys' room has an atmosphere all of its own. Amid the leather smell of saddles and boots, this is where jockeys retire to joke, argue, reflect on the previous event and gather their thoughts for the next, all while exchanging one set of silks for another.

I paused nervously in the doorway before being ushered into the room. Somebody must have mentioned that I rode a bit and had ambitions of becoming a jockey. One of the senior riders looked me up and down and said, 'Forget it, mate – you're too bloody big!'

The comment stung. The suggestion that I didn't have what it takes to make it as a jockey was like an instant red rag to a young bull. The rider hadn't meant to be unkind, but he didn't know me. Right there and then, I wanted nothing more in this world than to prove him wrong. Racing is a game of chance in all respects. But in my youthful determination this was a dead-set certainty. I would become a jockey. Nothing would stop me.

Looking back now I can understand that senior jockey's evaluation. He would have seen many young blokes of my height reach their late teens and fill out to a natural bodyweight that would preclude them from becoming a race rider. But what he didn't know was that my physiology would allow me to remain lean throughout my entire career, maintain my racing weight without severe fasting, and be able to eat just about anything my heart desired. I'd inherited my mum's light frame and kilojoule-burning metabolism. Without them, ability would have meant nothing. When you look at group photos of jockeys of my generation, I am usually the tallest of the bunch. As a kid, it had meant I was lean and strong. My genes dictated I would stay that way.

A significant number of young jockeys fail to see out their apprenticeships because of rising weight. Among those that do are plenty who spend their entire careers fasting, smoking, taking diuretics, purging, sweating in saunas and generally torturing themselves in the constant battle with weight. Research indicates that wasting can effect concentration and analytical skills. It can lead to depression and mood swings plus create all sorts of problems for your general health. I've no doubt that my natural good fortune in being able to maintain a regular weight without wasting has been a significant factor in my career, particularly in my success as a senior jockey.

Those considerations were a long way off when I presented myself at Terry Chinner's Gympie stables to begin my apprenticeship. Once again, the opportunity had come via my grandmother's racing connections and I jumped at the chance. It meant leaving home but, as a kid who had done a grown man's work for ages and had been relishing the prospect of independence, I was more than ready to be kicked out of the nest. So the move to Terry's Gympie stables was made with little fuss or fanfare.

In all of sport there is nothing quite like the relationship between trainer and jockey. Traditionally, it has been a master and man-servant relationship, one in which the trainer was boss in the strictest sense with the jockey little more than an underling doing his bidding. Of course, that old standard has been eroded over the years but even the most experienced and accomplished riders working in collaboration with a top mentor respect the fact that the trainer must be the boss. That said, for the latter part of my riding career, I have prided myself on doing my homework and have required very little instruction from a trainer as to how to get the best out of a certain horse.

My first contact with a trainer occurred when I was introduced to Terry Chinner at Gympie racetrack. Here I was, a 15-year-old runt, staring up at this big, bearded bloke who must have stood over 6 foot in his socks. An imposing presence!

The Chinners were a hardworking couple and wonderful horse people. The way they broke horses, educated them, handled and cared for the animals marked them as true horse lovers. I came to the stable with a good work ethic handed down from Tom Boss and Terry built on that. He instilled in me the lesson that if you wanted to carve out a life around horses you had to be prepared to work hard and never let up. Straightaway I settled into the routine of rising early to lay hands on rake, shovel, broom or bucket for the daily ritual of mucking out stalls and feeding and watering horses. The real attraction was the chance to exercise and ride track work on the quarter horses and thoroughbreds in Terry's care. With a few quiet tips from my master and by watching other riders, the rudiments of race riding soon clicked into place.

The Chinner stable was primarily involved in sprint racing, which involved racing quarter horses and/or thoroughbreds in the same field at registered race meetings. It is not a well-known pursuit in the capital cities but is popular in selected regional centres. Clubs like Gympie would put the sprint racing on at the end of the race program to encourage the punters to stay to the last event. Being indentured to a sprint-racing trainer meant my apprenticeship was vastly different to the city boys who were linked to stables based on the major metropolitan tracks. By comparison, mine was very rough and ready with plenty of my early riding done on the sand and soil surface of the Gympie track, rather than the lush turf of more salubrious settings.

It seems odd now, given how my life has worked out, but I have no recollection whatsoever of the moment that I first rode a thoroughbred. Those early weeks at the Chinner stables were a busy time, constantly working with and around horses, so much so that when the time came I paid no special heed as somebody, probably Terry, legged me up on to the back of a genuine racing thoroughbred to ride track work.

The greatest intellectual puzzle for a young apprentice is

how to calculate pace. It's easy in a motor car – you simply glance at the speedo. But on a racehorse, the jockey has to train his own inner computer to work out just how fast the animal beneath him is travelling. Too fast, and the horse will run out of gas before the race is done. Not fast enough, and you'll find yourself charging to the line with plenty left in the tank but too late to catch the leaders. All the great jockeys are fantastic judges of pace. I was never flash in maths at school but because the riddle of pace was a puzzle related to something I loved, it came to me pretty readily.

There was one hurdle that took a bit more conquering. For my entire life I'd always been relaxed around horses and had grown to understand that an animal picked up on that sense of calm and responded accordingly. It explained my affinity with them. But there was a hitch in this relationship between boy and beast that became apparent shortly after I started riding thoroughbreds in track work. Right from my early riding days, I had always felt that I was the master of affairs up there in the saddle. But the sheer power of the thoroughbred and the wild spirit that runs through the breed sowed a tiny granule of doubt in my mind: 'What if this thing just gets it into its head to bolt headlong, takes off like a scalded cat and just keeps going; what the hell could I do?'

At first it was just a random thought, but before too long it was recurring almost every time I walked a horse out to work.

The most prized quality of any trainer in the city or the bush is an educated eye. Terry Chinner spotted the problem as if he was reading my thoughts. And he had a solution. Without letting me know, one morning he legged me up on to a noted bolter. Barely had my bum touched the saddle when this thing took off like a runaway train. I could have thrown out

50 anchors but nothing was going to halt the headlong, blind, panicked flight as the crazed galloper tore around the track with me hanging on like a petrified rabbit. The fencing flew by. My mind was a blank as my greatest fear rolled out in super-fast motion. Surely we would go splintering through a rail to meet a gory end or smash horribly and fatally into an immovable object. None of that happened. In fact, nothing much at all really happened. Eventually, the horse began to tire and, sensing this, I simply eased him back under me and resumed control. It was one of the best lessons of my career and I have never forgotten it. To this day, I've had very few problems with bolting horses. Whenever a horse is inclined to bolt, I don't try to fight it. Instead, I let it have its head. I've grown to understand that one of horses' greatest fears is that they genuinely hate being out of control. After a few moments of having their head and sensing that lack of control, they actually welcome the gentle tightening of the rein to ease them back to placid compliance.

With that momentary phobia cured for good, I returned to my old confident ways around the horses. But, every now and then, they would deliver a reminder that they are incredibly strong, spirited animals, only a few heartbeats removed from the wild things that roamed the planet long before man made them a beast of burden and a form of entertainment.

I was in a stall performing a routine chore, my mind a million miles away, when a colt decided to let me know that I was on his turf and that he was definitely the boss. When stallions fight they look to get height over their opponent so they can use their weight and strength to bear down on their front legs and crush and subdue. And that's what this guy attempted to do to me. Distracted by my chores, I didn't see it coming. In a flash, he was up on his hind legs with his forelegs draped over my shoulders to bring me to the ground. Once he got me down I thought I was dead, as he was using his weight to kneel forward and pin me. But that's when the diminutive frame of a jockey can come in handy. Did I manage to wriggle out of there, or had the colt simply let me go, after having made his point and shown me who was in charge? I don't know, but one bruised and very shaken apprentice was wiser for the experience.

Life around the stables and riding track work kept me busy and taught me plenty. But the real reason I had left school and home at a tender age was to become a race rider. The image of that unforgettable afternoon at Gympie races was always running around inside my head and I wanted to bring it to life with me playing a feature role. At first I rode quarter horses. And then thoroughbreds. About eight months after joining the Chinner stables, I was legged up at Gympie for my first race start. I could barely believe it. The pony club kid had become a jockey, albeit an apprentice. And, just like at pony club, I started to win.

There was nothing earth-shattering about the fact that another country kid with a love of horses and a bit of competitive spirit was racking up a few wins on bush tracks. Promising kids come and go, some even win a few races until tougher competition, a fault in their technique or rising weight finds them out. I vowed that none of that was going to happen to me. In reality, I was a rough-arsed country kid riding on modest bush tracks. But in my mind the picture was altogether different. To me, the race rides weren't on battling provincial campaigners but on glamorous champions. The venue wasn't a bush track but somewhere like Randwick, Flemington or Moonee Valley. Champions aren't meant to lose, and nor were my mounts. Sports psychologists call it positive visualisation but I was simply living out a wonderful fantasy and, in so doing, moving heaven and earth to convert my rides into winners.

My two favourite videos were highlight reels of the superstars of the day – The King and The Man: Kingston Town and Manikato. With Gary Willetts in the saddle Manikato was like a Formula One racer in a field of shopping trolleys. When heads were turned for home, you'd wait until the race caller said '. . . and here comes Manikato' and you would know it was all over. At his best he was unstoppable, winning the Futurity Stakes at Caulfield Racecourse four times and the weight-for-age William Reid at Moonee Valley an incredible five times. As a two-year-old in 1978 he won both the Blue Diamond at Caulfield and the Golden Slipper at Rosehill. As a three-year-old he won eight of his 12 starts. Good judges almost wrote him off when a bleeding problem and leg injuries interrupted his career. But, even below his best, The Man was still good enough to win 12 and be placed in nine of his remaining 22 starts.

And then there was The King. Trained by the great Tommy Smith, Kingston Town dominated the 1980s, winning 30 of his 41 starts and becoming the first galloper in Australasia to plunder a million dollars in prize money. In Sydney he was virtually unbeatable. But it was at Moonee Valley, where he was shooting for an unprecedented third Cox Plate, that he truly claimed his place in Australian sporting folklore. At the 600-metre mark, the prince of race callers Bill Collins uttered the immortal words, 'Kingston Town cannot win . . .' before describing to an incredulous audience how the mighty black gelding swamped a crack field over the last two furlongs (400 metres) to win the weight-for-age crown for the third time. Brilliance and toughness in the one package – what a racehorse!

Those highlight tapes of The King and The Man were played, rewound and played again until they were all but worn out. But it wasn't just the horses that inspired me. My role model of the time was Kingston Town's regular race rider Malcolm Johnston. Here was a jockey who not only brought brilliance to the craft but added a huge dash of personality. He was cheeky, opinionated, always had a ready smile for the fans and a great quote for the media. They say you shouldn't meet your idols because they are always doomed to disappoint. Not so Malcolm Johnston. When I met him some years later, I found him an ever-friendly, extremely approachable horseman always willing to assist a young jockey with encouragement or advice. And boy, could he ride. I devoured videos of him in action, adapting elements of his technique to my own riding style. People ask me who had the greatest influences on my development as a jockey. The truth is I learned much of what I know from observing others, adapting ideas, experimenting and finally incorporating whatever worked best for me. Malcolm Johnston's style was definitely in that mix. As a jockey, you never stop learning, never stop making small adjustments in the quest for perfection.

Many jockeys get their start in provincial racing. The talented ones work their way to the big cities and eventually ride in Group events, the forum for quality gallopers. Group 1 is the highest level, attracts the best horses and offers the largest stake money. It is racing's showcase.

My dreams of riding Group 1 winners on the great tracks

of Australia were alive in my head but first I had to survive my initiation to the riding ranks. If you don't have what it takes to become a jockey, an apprenticeship will soon sort you out. Traditionally, the time a young apprentice spends indentured to his master is not meant to be easy. Come race day, a jockey is entrusted to pilot a valuable thoroughbred, the property of owners who deserve to see that animal perform at its best. The horse will carry the financial support of punters who can be unforgiving of a rider who falls short of their expectations. During his apprenticeship a jockey must learn the rudiments of race riding and he must also learn respect. Along the way, he will rise many hours before the rest of the world, work hard and do it without complaint, day after day. The master is looking for the apprentice with the right blend of ability, determination, respect and work ethic to go the distance.

Senior jockeys like to outdo each other on stories about the toughness of their apprenticeships. But surely the prize for the best yarn must go to Darren Beadman. He was indentured to one of the game's greatest mentors, Theo Green, a caring but nonetheless strict disciplinarian who shaped the careers of some of the nation's finest race riders. Theo had a reputation for turning out future champion jockeys but getting into or out of his stable was no easy matter. Darren reckoned that Theo worked his boys so hard that they would have done anything for a day off. In fact, Darren did. He turned up at a hospital insisting he had appendicitis. There was absolutely nothing wrong with his health, but having a bodily organ removed was the only way he could 'legitimately' score a few days break from Theo's ruthless regimen.

My tutelage was happening a long way from the glamour stables of Randwick and Flemington. But I didn't mind. Racing lore held that rural Queensland was one of the great breeding grounds for champion jockeys and my dreams of making it big in the city were undiminished by opportunity or distance.

With that sort of ambition, winning seemed to come easy. On one exhilarating afternoon at Gympie, I almost won every race I rode, which is called 'riding the card'. It was a five-race program, I won four and was nutted by a nose in the other. The winners kept piling up with such frequency that by the end of my first full racing year I had run away with both the apprentice and senior jockeys' titles at Gympie.

This form hadn't escaped the attention of race steward Graham Ireland. A former top jockey, there wasn't much he didn't know about the game and after noting my progress and knowing that I still had much to learn, made the gentle observation that a change of scene might do me the world of good.

'You've done just about all you can do here,' he said. 'I reckon it's time to move on.'

I thought about what he had said. Perhaps it was time to enter the second phase of my jockey education. A move to a more competitive environment might be just what I needed to assist my development and, although I wouldn't have admitted it, get my attitude knocked into shape. Maybe the business of riding winners had come too easily for me. Looking back now, I can see that my ultra-competitiveness had developed nasty side effects. To my ambition and hard-working ways I had added cockiness and an abrasive edge. Phone calls were made, deals struck. I was on my way out of Gympie and the Terry Chinner stable. The Gold Coast had better look out!

3
Luck's a fortune

It was hardly the entry of a conquering hero. The boy from the bush arrived at south-east Queensland's famous coastal strip driving a car down the wrong side of the Gold Coast Highway. In my rural existence I hadn't struck too many divided roads and didn't realise that one set of lanes carried only southbound traffic while another set catered for motorists heading north. No wonder freaked-out drivers were flashing their lights and swerving to get out of the way!

It had been quite a departure from Gympie. My leaving hadn't been as pleasant as I would have liked. There had been some disagreement about my entitlements and, by way of compensation, I had accepted an offer of a car in lieu of payment. It didn't make my mood any brighter when I later found out there was money still owing on the second-hand banger. So, despite my modest success in the saddle, I was virtually penniless. There wasn't even enough money in my wallet to buy gas for the drive to the Gold Coast.

But, as everybody in the racing game comes to understand, luck's a fortune. Not for the last time in my life would I recognise the hand of Lady Luck trumping in at the right time to bail me out of tight spot. On the point of despair over my cash-strapped situation, I suddenly remembered how I had stashed away a sling from one of my favourite owners, a bloke who had funded his modest racing ambitions from sapphire mining. Instead of slipping me a cash bonus, he had passed me a fistful of the blue stones with the tip: 'Hang on to these, they'll be worth a bit of money one day.'

No matter how desperate my financial situation, I had never thought about selling the stones before. They were a charm, a reminder of my rough and ready initiation to the racing game, my passage from boyhood to the working world. When it came time to leave, I balanced those blue chips in my hand, weighing up what to do. The answer was simple: despite that miner's advice to hang on to the rocks, I had to convert some of them to cash. Call it an investment in my future. Instead of driving straight to the Gold Coast, I took a detour and headed up into the hinterland hill country to the town of Mapleton. Somebody had told me there was a gem trader up there. The tiny blue stones turned out to be one of the best slings of all. There was no way I could part with all the rocks, so I handed over just a few in exchange for a couple of thousand dollars. With a full tank of gas, a meal in my stomach and some travelling cash in my wallet, I finally pointed that old banger downhill towards the coast. To this day, along with my most treasured riding mementoes, I still have the remainder of those sapphires among my keepsakes.

Kaye Tinsley had a real presence about him. The Kiwi horse-man had left behind a distinguished career as one of New Zealand's top jockeys to try his hand at the training game. In his middle years, his lightweight jockey frame had filled out into a solid, stocky physique that exuded strength and a no-nonsense approach to all things. It was an impression supported by the firmness of his handshake and the way he looked me straight in the eye at our first meeting. Nominating Kaye as my new master had been Graham Ireland's call. Maybe he had thought: 'I know just the bloke to put a tight rein on this headstrong kid from Caboolture.' He had chosen well. The plan was for me to live with Kaye and his wife Chick at their family home not far from the Gold Coast track. Their grown daughter Tania had moved out so there was room at the inn.

As opposed to the towering Terry Chinner Kaye was shorter than me but sure made up for it with the size of his personality. As I would soon learn, Kaye would never leave you wondering what he was thinking. He was always straightforward and would cut to the chase in an instant. At that stage of my career, as a strong-willed teenager living away from home, I needed a good disciplinarian, a hard boss – and Kaye was just the man.

The Tinsleys were a great team. Kaye was the horseman and Chick was just about everything else. She was a wonderful woman with great motherly instincts and an incredible work ethic. Whether around the stables or taking care of the accounts, Chick never stopped. Everything about the Gold Coast setup was on a different scale to what I had encountered in Gympie. For starters, Kaye had about 40 horses in work. In the first 18 months of my apprenticeship I had done a bit of track work but nothing compared with what I was about to take on for Kaye and other trainers. From jumping up on just a few horses during my working week, I moved straight into riding about 12 or 15 thoroughbreds each morning. It was a huge learning curve and I really enjoyed it. My appetite for riding as much as possible was a bonus that really accelerated my education. On a daily basis I was learning more and more about the craft. My routine was to rise just after 3 am, do my chores and then get down the track to ride work for either Kaye, John Wallace, Noel Doyle or any of the other trainers prepared to entrust me with their horses.

Kaye was a terrific boss, tough but always fair. He made me work extremely hard but that was okay by me because that's how I'd been brought up. But one characteristic that had me scratching my head was his habit on race day of rarely putting his apprentices on horses he trained. Instead, he usually gave the rides to senior jockeys. It wasn't because he thought I was a dud rider. In fact, I rode a winner for him at my very first Gold Coast meeting. Later, when I was riding in Brisbane with some success he still never gave me the pick of his horses. Maybe he thought he was doing me a favour by creating the opportunity to ride as often as possible for more powerful stables. As puzzled as I was by this development, I didn't let it get me down but used it to spread myself around and show other trainers that I was willing to have a go.

I might have been a country boy but the Gold Coast was a comfortable fit. If the challenge of race riding had found me out of my depth and struggling, things might have been different. But right from the outset, I started riding winners. The local view when I first arrived on the Coast was that this Boss kid was a bit of a rough nut who had been brought up on quarter horses rather than thoroughbreds, and that he would need a few edges knocked off him. They may have been right. But I caught on quick and the prospect of riding so much track work created a steep learning curve that the new kid in town was more than willing to shimmy up as fast as he could.

If Kaye wasn't putting me on his best it didn't matter. Other trainers were more than pleased with my work. The offers kept coming and so did the winners. My short-term plan had been to restrict myself to the Gold Coast until I was settled but opportunity soon took me farther afield. At first it was the provincial tracks nearby – Murwillumbah across the border in New South Wales, or Beaudesert.

However, as my form continued to improve and the winners kept stepping up, the big smoke beckoned. Brisbane. A year after my move from Gympie I was riding on metropolitan tracks in the Queensland capital. The surroundings were flasher, the standard higher and the crowds bigger. But I wasn't intimidated. Success certainly made a difference. As happened when I landed on the Coast, I rode a winner at my first outing in the big smoke. It might have only been a midweek meeting but returning to scale that day at Eagle Farm had me daring to believe that my vision of booting home winners on big tracks was something more than the idle dreams of a country kid with delusions of grandeur.

By the end of that first year I was riding all of my track work on the Gold Coast but concentrating more of my race riding efforts on Brisbane. On Thursdays it was nearby Ipswich; on Saturdays Eagle Farm or Doomben. That first win in the city was special and, thankfully, it wasn't a flash in the pan. The winners kept coming and so did the slings from grateful owners. Apprentices are obliged to pay a considerable share of their race proceeds to their masters, but I was going well enough to guarantee that there was always a bit left in my wallet.

Being dropped into a new environment can be a bit unsettling but, despite my raw bush ways, I had fitted into the Gold Coast lifestyle like a backside in a bucket. From growing up on a farm I had slipped into the suburban stream and become a city kid. You can take the boy out of the bush, they say, but you can't take the bush out of the boy. That remains true to this day. But it sure pays to be adaptable and make the most of whatever situation comes your way. There was nothing better than driving back from Brisbane late on a Saturday afternoon after booting home a couple of winners, with a few healthy slings in my wallet and the prospect of stepping out on the town that night to celebrate. Pre-Gold Coast, my boots had slipped into plenty of riding irons but they had never stepped through the front door of a pub, let alone a nightclub with flashing lights, loud music and girls. What I'm going to say next is not news to anyone close to the racing game but it still bears saying. Jockeys are usually cocky little buggers. Who can blame us? It takes a bit of nerve for guys with tiny builds to jump up on powerful thoroughbreds and ride them like your life depends on it. Naturally, successful jockeys like to strut their stuff. So, here I was, all of 18, hitting the high spots of the Coast. Me and my new-found jockey mates were a competitive bunch. We competed for the best clothes and fancied ourselves as the best movers on the dance floor and the best drinkers at the bar. With a bit of cash in our pockets we lived it up like big shots. Time would reveal to me that, the world over, young jockeys are pretty much the same. We were following a time-honoured ritual of cutting our teeth and trying to let everybody, including ourselves, know that we were going okay.

We were cheeky fellas, mischievous, gave anyone and everyone a hard time or a bit of lip. It was all in good fun. Back then, you could get away with it. Today, somebody might take it the wrong way. The Coast is full of characters and many of them come out after dark to frequent the night spots. I enjoyed their company and the vibrant nightlife. Who needed sleep? At 18 or 19 you can just keep bouncing, and we did, often going straight from a nightclub to track work, and then sleeping the rest of the afternoon. We thought we were big shots but, really, we were just a bunch of kids making our way.

If at any stage I looked like getting too far ahead of myself, the powerful hand of Kaye Tinsley was there to pull me back into line. As an ex-jockey, he knew exactly what we were like and, on the odd occasion, we locked horns. Both he and Chick came with an attitude that was second to none. Not only was Kaye tireless, he did everything to perfection. From the second he started with the horses each morning until he fell into bed that night, every task that Kaye performed was absolutely spot on. Nobody left until the job was done to his satisfaction. In all ways he was hard but fair. At times I thought he was pretty tough on me, but looking back now I can see that he was exactly the sort of boss this Boss needed.

At that stage, with a few bob in my pocket and a bit of success on the track, I had a touch of the lair in me and might have gone down the wrong path. Kaye Tinsley kept me on the straight and narrow. As I said, I'd always been a bit of a perfectionist when it comes to work but, back then, I wasn't in the same league as Kaye. In my haste to consume as much of life as possible, sometimes I would rush my chores. Kaye would grab me by the ear, make me do them again and reinforce the value of doing all things right in the first place. 'If you realised you should do it properly first time,' he'd say, 'you'd get it down half as quick.' He was merely defining the boundaries all of us need as we grow.

4
Fame, fortune . . . and bankruptcy

There was another stabilising force about to appear on my horizon, one that would prove the greatest anchor in my life. It was racing carnival time on the Gold Coast, a chance for the place and its people to throw on the glad rags, party a bit more and enjoy a day at the races with the prospect of real atmosphere and quality fields. That's when I first saw her – at the track, a face in the crowd. She was all of 16, I was 18. I learned that her name was Sloane Gavin. And if it wasn't love at first sight on my part, it was probably the next best thing. Sloane took my eye straightaway. I recognised the family name, and knew her mum and dad, Grant and Wendy, were race regulars and that her elder sister Gianne had a share in a horse. At the end of the day, I was driving out of the course when I spotted Gianne and a girlfriend waiting for a cab. I stopped and offered them a lift down to the Gavin family home at Burleigh Heads. We got to talking on the way and I asked after

Sloane. The girls mentioned that they were going to Fortunes nightclub at Jupiters Casino that night and asked if I would like to come. Sloane would be there. We all met up later that night. I danced with Sloane, had a few drinks and a chat.

> SLOANE: 'We were very young. You tend to take things as they come when you're that age. It was a great night. We talked and got on very well. I don't remember either of us being stuck for words. Everything seemed so easy. It just seemed so natural.'

We clicked. It was as simple and beautiful as that. Since that night we have barely spent more than a day apart. But, I must tell you, I almost blew it. On parting that Saturday evening, I asked if we could catch up on the Sunday. The only problem was I couldn't remember exactly whereabouts in Burleigh they lived. I spent the day driving around fruitlessly trying to identify streets and houses. I had stupidly forgotten to ask Sloane for a phone number so there was no way I could have contacted her. Humiliated, I turned the car around and slunk out of Burleigh wondering if I had wrecked my chances from the outset. I hadn't. We hooked up again the following Saturday and had a great time. My male pride stopped me from telling her how I had mucked up our date the previous Sunday, but when we had known each other long enough and could laugh about it, I confessed.

It was obvious very early in the piece that she was the one for me. We were easy in each other's company, never ran out of things to talk about and did everything together. It's still the same today.

When I had first arrived on the Coast, I lived with Kaye and

Chick at their family home. But later they created a self-contained pad for me above the stables. It was like a loft studio and at first I loved it and the sense of independence that went with it. The only problem was that the party gang thought it was pretty cool too. When I was in Brisbane at a race meeting, they would gather there on a Saturday afternoon prior to us stepping out on the town. By the time I arrived home, they would have eaten most of my food and be wearing half of my wardrobe. Now, I was pretty house proud. I'd do the washing, stock the fridge, leave the place clean. When I'd get home from the races, it would all be gone, as the party gang had scoffed the lot. They would cook up a feed and never clean up after themselves. What's more, if they wanted a shirt for Saturday night they would have a rummage through my closet. It was amazing. I never blew up at them but hoped that somebody would get the message and chip in. They never did. It was a losing proposition. I tolerated this at first but after a few too many trips to the supermarket to replenish the grocery supply, being left to tidy up after their departure and wash the clothes that they had worn and discarded, it all became a bit of a pain in the butt. I was looking forward to when my apprenticeship finished and my choice of domestic situation would be my own.

Sloane's parents knew I wasn't happy and when the odd sleepover at their place grew into a semi-permanent arrangement, they were sympathetic hosts. But I had created a problem for myself and it was about to bite hard. The conditions of my apprenticeship were that I was meant to reside at accommodation provided by my master, so in the wee small hours I would motor back to the stables, douse the lights, switch the car off and glide stealthily into my parking spot before starting work for the day. My boss was many things, but he was no fool. He knew that I was up to something. One afternoon he sat in his car at a convenient spot and watched me head off to Burleigh. Next morning, when I glided silently into my parking spot at the stables, he was waiting for me. And I wasn't going to be let off with a mere warning. Kaye wanted to teach me a lesson. He took me before the presiding body who demonstrated just how grossly I had breached the terms of my apprenticeship by suspending me from riding for a couple of months.

The first thing I did when I finished my apprenticeship was to rent an apartment. I loved the Burleigh area near Sloane's family home so we picked out a handy unit, leased a pile of furniture, slapped down the bond plus a month or so in advance and moved in.

During his apprenticeship, a young rider's winnings from race placings are held in trust until he graduates as a senior jockey. On receipt of my entitlement, I went out and brought a brand new Toyota Celica for 30-odd thousand dollars. With the start-up costs on the new apartment plus the car, it was quite a considerable outlay but what the heck, I was a successful jockey, wasn't I? But just when Sloane and I should have been strolling happily into the future, we copped the biggest kick in the pants of our young lives. My independence had come at quite a price. To help establish my career, I had engaged the services of an accountant. He called us in to a meeting and the news was all bad. It seems that during the first half of my apprenticeship days going all the way back to Gympie, I had missed the lesson about making regular contributions to the Australian Tax Office. The accountant showed me what I owed and my jaw dropped. With all the fines for late payment included, it was more than I had left in my bank account. Even

when he negotiated with the ATO about my particular circumstances and had the figure reduced, it was the equivalent of all
the cash we had left. They gave us next to no time to pay and
the prospect of facing further penalties if we didn't. We were
cleaned out. Broke.

We drove back to our new home in silence, two chickens
busted at the first foray out of the nest. I felt terrible. After all,
it was my tax bill, not Sloane's. We didn't even have enough for
a bag of groceries. I went downstairs and scraped about in
the ashtray, console and glove box of the Celica until I found
enough coins to buy some milk, bread and a newspaper. The
latter was the most important because I needed to confirm my
races. I came back upstairs and said to Sloane: 'Today is the day
we either go back to your mum and dad's place or I go to the
races and ride a winner.' Privately, I was thinking, 'This is a
make or break day.' Moving back to Sloane's family home
wouldn't be such a bad option, but I was a man who had made
a play by moving out into the world and I didn't want to turn
tail at this point.

So much for the image of the successful jockey. Besides the
car, we had nothing to our names. The flat was rented and so
was the furniture. I climbed behind the wheel of the car, pointed
its nose towards Ipswich races and thought: 'Here goes.'

It was a good day. No, it was more than a good day. It was
one of those turning points. I had been booked for three rides
and they all won. Copped a couple of healthy slings too.
Interestingly, the race club used to pay cash for riding fees and
percentages. The jockeys would line up outside the secretary's
office and receive cash in the hand. I drove home that night
with a cool 1200 bucks in my wallet. It was a massive relief. We
were back! I grabbed Sloane and we went out to dinner.

On the following Saturday, I rode two more winners and paid the rent. We were back on the bike. That old chestnut about what doesn't kill you makes you stronger sure rang true that week. It showed me that in Sloane I had found somebody who would stick fast through thick and thin. It also gave me a glimpse into the relationship between pressure and performance. Later in life I would understand that when the pressure is at its greatest, it sure sharpens the focus. In time I would learn to welcome the pressure as a friend. When you rise to the challenge you get to be your best.

That lesson rode with me like a saddlecloth. It's not like I go to bed every night thinking about it but, when the time comes – when I'm cornered – I can often pull out the sort of performance that turns a losing proposition into a winner. One example of this was the first time I left Australia to ride in Hong Kong as a senior jockey. I quickly realised that I was pretty much alone in an ultra-competitive environment and nobody was about to do me any favours. You've never seen jockeys undermine each other for rides until you've encountered it Hong Kong-style. It was ruthless and a real shock to a bloke from laidback Australia. For anyone not doing well, it can seem like the loneliest place in the world. When, for the umpteenth time, a trainer took me off a ride for no apparent reason, I blew up. Nobody enjoys being treated like a second-rate idiot. I made a promise: 'I swear to God, if I don't ride a winner tomorrow, I'm going home.'

The next day, I rode a treble. Again, I was out of the corner and on a roll.

Those defining moments crop up from time to time. Is it luck or really a matter of pulling one rein and backing that call with everything you've got? It was like the day I went up to the hills to cash in those sapphires. It was a time to be decisive. Maybe I am like that cat who looks like it's heading for a cropper but at the last moment manages to land on its feet. When somebody takes me off a horse, I often end up with a better ride. Once a door is closed, my attention swings 100 per cent to finding a new, better option. By instinct, I've always refused to settle for second-best. How did that habit form? I don't know. It was never like I had a particular mentor who drummed the message into me.

Many people, particularly in the racing business, tend to talk it up – make promises that they can't keep. I was brought up to believe that it's embarrassing to say something and then not follow it up with the action. If I tell people I'm going to do something, then I do it. Respect was a word that kept cropping up during my upbringing – respect your elders, your family, your job, your peers. But, most of all, respect yourself. Respecting yourself meant not letting yourself down when given a responsibility. As a kid, I tried to do my jobs to perfection. When slashing a paddock, the tractor wheel would be exactly on the last cutting line to ensure that there wasn't a single blade of grass missed in the process. Washing a car meant much more than a lick and a promise. Was it a matter of bringing those simple values into my career? Probably. If you are going to do something that's important to you, better that you give it a red-hot go than die wondering just how good you might have been.

The Gold Coast was good to me. All these years later I always make a point of returning there, visiting old haunts, catching up with friends and making new ones. It's the sort of place where people are larger than life and have a genuine crack at making a go of things. I met Billy Cross on the Coast. As soon-to-be-mates, we made an odd pair. I was a jockey and Billy was a former bricklayer who had graduated to perform in the male strip troupe known as Manpower. But there was much more to him than a cut torso. In fact, he ended up buying the Manpower concept and turning it into an international entertainment concern. It was soon evident he had the golden touch for business. Like riding horses, it's all about touch and timing and Billy had it in spades. His business mushroomed into an entertainment empire comprising nightclubs, bars, touring acts and shows big and bold enough to command long-term bookings in Las Vegas.

Billy would never rest on his laurels. Instead, he soaked up new ideas, travelled overseas to evaluate the latest trends in the show-business world and brought the best back home. In that way, his businesses have continued to evolve, change and stay ahead of the game.

By reputation, entertainment impresarios have flash personalities. But Billy is the most humble, down-to-earth bloke you could ever meet. We talk about twice a week and it is always a treat to hear his up-tempo, positive approach to all things. Like me, Billy understands the value of making a decision and giving it 100 per cent to make it work. You can go through life and meet a few people who you really trust, who will be there through thick and thin. That's me and Billy – a friendship forever.

Like Billy Cross, two characters who richly deserved a return on their investment in life were the former Billabong surfwear boys, brothers Scott and Matt Perrin. I came to know the Gold

Coast natives as lawyers who had been beavering away in the banking and finance investment sector for a fair time. In 1985, the Perrins' love affair with thoroughbreds took flight when they led in their first winner.

In 1998, the Perrins bought a half share in surf clothing firm Billabong for $26.4 million. At the time the company had annual revenue of $64.5 million. When they cashed up and left four years later, revenue had hit $490 million a year.

Scottie Perrin became a mate of mine and I soon developed a high regard for the cool way he went about making the world of business sound every bit as exciting as horse racing. We would talk on a daily basis about what he was trying to achieve, as well as horses. He was investing a fortune in the racing game and my fervent wish was to be the jockey who would be a part of their success.

It has taken me a long time to acquire such friendships. I don't treat them lightly. Once I strike a friendship, the world would move on its axis before we would cross swords. As a boy growing up I learned the value of an old Australian saying: 'Your mates are your mates'. Enough said.

My time riding on the Gold Coast delivered two apprentice premierships and gave me the chance on some terrific horses. One was a gutsy mare called Bassie's Pride. She didn't know how to quit and together we won seven races. Another was Rancho Classic, a galloper who helped put me on the map when trainer Howard Wilson took me to Hawkesbury on Sydney's north-western fringe where we won the 1990 Gold Cup. At that point, Rancho Classic was the finest horse I had ridden.

For the final stretch of my apprenticeship, when I graduated to the senior ranks, I was riding full-time in Brisbane and doing pretty damn well. My record shows that I never won a Brisbane jockeys' premiership and, although I wouldn't admit it at the time, that was largely my own fault. Brisbane was a competitive market where brilliant jockeys like Mick Dittman, Ken Russell and Shane Scriven made it hard for any individual to dominate. But I didn't need other riders bringing me undone – I was my own worst enemy. That ultra-competitive streak that Graham Ireland had spotted back in Gympie had followed me all the way to the big smoke with the usual nasty side effects sure to land me in trouble. The upside of my win-at-all-costs attitude was plenty of race winners. The downside was way too many suspensions – at least six or eight a year. Racing is a strictly policed business. At one stage or another every jockey cops a rap on the knuckles from the stewards. Some more than others. You don't win premierships sitting on the sidelines.

Ambition is a noble quality, but it can have an ugly side. My competitive nature was so strong and my self-belief so complete that the issue of not winning brought out the very worst in me. Whenever I was on a horse that didn't share my ambition to be first past the post, my intolerance would boil over. During his apprenticeship a jockey is taught to be respectful of owners, trainers and race officials. The owners, in particularly, are the very lifeblood of the sport. Whether their horse is a champion or a bush nag, they deserve to be treated with courtesy and respect. As a teenager, this was a lesson I had yet to learn. The punters and most trainers appreciated my desire to win but there were others not so taken by my style. Growing up I had always been a bit blunt – a characteristic of a bush upbringing where you tell it like it is. It pays to be honest, but sometimes being brutally honest can be a real pain in the neck.

On returning to the enclosure on a runner that had fallen short of my ruthless expectations, instead of offering some consoling words to the disappointed owners, I would often tell them in the most blunt fashion exactly what they should do with their untalented pride and joy. There are plenty of diplomatic ways to tell owners their galloper doesn't quite have what it takes. Instead, I'd give it to them right between the eyes. The worse thing I said to an owner was, 'If you want a ticket to the races, just ring me up and I'll get you one. But don't bring your bloody horse!' Older jockeys and trainers would look at me and shake their heads in horror. But I paid them no heed.

That abrasive, ultra-competitive nature was bound to land me in strife. Winning to me was everything and out on the track my job was to give my horse every chance – even if that meant ruffling a few feathers. The stewards didn't necessarily see it that way. Sure, I was booting home plenty of winners and starting to earn a few write-ups in the local papers but I was also upsetting people, including rival jockeys and race stewards. It was a case of three steps forward and two steps back as my chances of riding more winners were impeded by a series of suspensions handed down by the stewards. Rather than accept these rulings with contrition and an undertaking to mend my ways, I'd leave each inquiry in a seething rage, convinced I was the victim of a gross miscarriage of justice. In my mind I was right and they were wrong.

That sort of attitude is bound to create a bit of froth and bubble and word soon got around that this Boss kid was a hothead. Sloane recognised it and, in the nicest way, told me I needed to pull my head in. But I wasn't listening. You might say

I was way too temperamental. If I rode two winners, instead of celebrating that success, I'd be filthy about being beaten on another two that might have won. 'I should have had four,' I'd be saying to myself, stewing about the ones that got away. It was an attitude that would persist for years. This wasn't Caboolture Pony Club where just about every ribbon and trophy finished up on my shelf. This was the big world of thoroughbred racing and I was yet to understand that I couldn't win every race. Racing is a game where chance plays an enormous part. Sometimes you are bound to lose. If you have 25 rides a week, the law of averages says there will always be a few unlucky ones. It's just the nature of the game. It would take a me a long while to learn that lesson. Today, I'm still just as passionate but I know how to keep the disappointments under wraps and how to enjoy the success when it comes.

But back then, as quick as I was picking up tips to make me a smarter rider, I was equally slow in learning how to play the game out of the saddle. When hauled before the stewards I was certain that I was never wrong.

The Doomben 10,000 is one of the biggest races on the Queensland turf calendar, a major Group 1 event with the sort of cache and stake money to attract the best stables and thoroughbreds from Sydney. I had every reason to believe the 10,000 in 1994 would be the most important race of my young career. Rather than the race ride going to one of the big guns from down south, trainer Lee Freedman had elected me to ride the brilliant filly Bint Marscay, winner of the Golden Slipper the previous year. It was my very first ride for Lee and I was keen to impress. By then I knew the Doomben track like the home paddock back in Caboolture. I was improving my position in the race when I shifted Bint Marscay for a run. The only problem was that there was another horse on the inside. To this day I feel that the senior jockey riding that horse used me up. He stayed there too long in order to get a better position. The stewards would later rule that I wasn't clear of the trailing horse when I shifted. The move created a chain reaction causing a fall back in the field. In the charge to the post Bint Marscay was beaten by a nostril by a horse called Flitter, in what would have been my first Group 1 victory. What was almost a good day's work soured on the way back to the enclosure when we learned that two horses had fallen. In the subsequent enquiry it was deemed to be my fault and the stewards slapped me with a two-month suspension for careless riding. It was an ugly scene inside the steward's room – Chief Steward Ray Murrihy presiding over a serious matter and an angry jockey totally convinced that he was blameless and about to become the victim of a gross miscarriage of justice. The matter would drag its way through a series of appeals which I was always destined to lose.

When the final verdict was handed down I went ballistic and it took the best efforts of Brisbane's leading turf writer Bart Sinclair to drag me out of the room before I shredded what was left of my career. They then hit me with an extra month for misconduct. It was to prove a very expensive lesson. In all, I would be out for a total of 29 race meetings, not to mention the legal bills I had incurred throughout the appeals process. What a shambles – my first ride for Lee Freedman and I end up in the stewards room defending myself on a serious careless riding charge!

Today, I can see that I wasn't clear when I shifted. But, back then, the bull-headed young man would never admit he was wrong. In my fury and frustration I had become totally convinced that the Brisbane racing authorities, as epitomised by Ray Murrihy, had it in for me. We had locked horns on way too many occasions. You could say that the relationship between the Queensland Turf Club's Chief Steward and myself had developed into a major personality clash. Now, who do you think was going to win that battle – the suspended hothead stewing on the sidelines for three months, or the chief steward calmly going about his business of trying to keep the game on the straight and narrow? I was all of 23 with a black-and-white view of the world: they were wrong, I was right. I still had plenty to learn.

After that, there was no way I could continue in Brisbane. In fact, as far as I was concerned, they could jam the entire racing scene where the sun doesn't shine. 'See ya later, boys,' I resolved. 'I'm off to Sydney!'

I was on the quickest route out of town but not before giving the Brisbane racing environment and the people who ran it the biggest parting spray I could muster. The media quotes were not directed at the racing public, trainers or owners but at the authorities and I left them in no doubt of my contempt for them. It was the rant of an immature and self-absorbed young man but, back then, I was absolutely certain I was right. However, it is never too late to apologise and admit that you were wrong. In time, Ray Murrihy would re-locate to Sydney to become Chief Steward at the Australian Jockey Club and he and I were destined to get along famously and develop a great mutual respect.

In many ways, my timing for leaving couldn't have been worse. Sloane and I had just built our waterfront dream home on a canal development on the Gold Coast. It was brand new, we had just moved in and Sloane had every right to be looking

forward to years of domestic bliss under its roof. I stormed
home from the final losing appeal to announce that I would be
moving to Sydney as soon as possible and leaving Sloane with
the task of packing up the house and arranging the move.
Today, I can't believe how irrational and unfair that sounds but
to her eternal credit, Sloane didn't even blink. Events had taken
a radical turn neither of us could have envisaged but my partner simply took it in her stride with her customary attitude of
making the best of whatever befell us.

Making big decisions on impulsive, hot-headed whims is not
the way to plan your life. But, as the old saying goes, 'It's not
what happens . . . It's what happens next.' There was no back-
tracking on the brash resolution to uproot my career from the
safe haven of Brisbane and the Gold Coast and head off to
the ultra-competitive Sydney racing environment. I put my head
down and resolved to make the best of it.

5

Past the post

My first call was to Max Lees, the leading Newcastle trainer with a terrific record in Sydney and for whom I had previously ridden plenty of winners, including a Group 2 victory on a horse called Double Your Bet.

'Would you put me on if I moved to Sydney?' I asked Max.

'Get on the next plane,' was his curt reply. It was the winter of 1993 and my sentence still had a long way to run so there was no way I could do any race riding. But there was always track work and the task of building the sort of relationships with owners and trainers that would prove invaluable once my suspension time was up. The contacts I had made on previous trips to Sydney would come in very handy. At carnival time I had often travelled south with Gold Coast trainer Noel Doyle. We would stay at Warwick Farm and it was there that I got to know Clarry Connors, who was enjoying a golden run as a trainer at the time. Among his string was a filly I had ridden in her first race start and immediately declared that she could win the Golden Slipper. Just before Christmas, Clarry had phoned to say that the filly, whose name was Burst, was back in work and asked whether I was coming down. I was back in Brisbane riding winners and had declined the opportunity. From that point until the end of autumn she won at every start, including the Golden Slipper. After placing that first call to Max Lees, I phoned Clarry. Obviously, he had forgiven my previous poor judgement because he promised to put me on if I moved to Sydney.

Encouraged, I kissed Sloane goodbye, and set off into the great unknown of the next big challenge of my professional life. I had arranged to hook up with a couple of friends who would show me around until I could navigate my own way through the Sydney street system. There was no time to waste sight-seeing. I had come to work.

The leading trainers and stable foremen know their racing history. They are all aware of the great riding heritage that took a procession of jockeys from the Queensland bush all the way to Royal Randwick, Flemington and even Royal Ascot. It was a heritage which embraced a conga line of talent and included two geniuses of the turf – Neville Sellwood and George Moore. It also included the brilliant Darby McCarthy, a bush natural who was already riding winners at Cunnamulla and Thargomindah when he was 12 and went on to star in Europe and England. The Sydney racing mob knew I could ride and were willing to give me a go.

Barely had my boots touched down in the harbour city than I was riding track work for a growing list of mentors including Les Bridge, Bart Cummings and Gai Waterhouse.

SLOANE: 'When Glen announced he was going to Sydney, deep down I thought it wouldn't last long. After all, we had just moved into our new home. I'd always thought that Sydney was where Shane Dye and Darren Beadman were the top riders. It wasn't a place for boys from the Queensland bush. We'd seen other Queensland riders go down there for to give it a go before returning home. Plenty had tried but few had stuck it out. Then he rang to say he was getting rides for people like Gai Waterhouse.'

There was no lag-time. Straightaway I was into the groove, working hard and riding as many horses as possible. Again, the timing was good. The suspension had been handed down in winter which meant my return occurred in spring when all the best riders were down south for the Melbourne carnival. It meant plenty of work and plenty of rides for me with the major stables. That spring, in the space of four or five weeks, I was well and truly back riding winners. Trainers reward good form. Their regard for my riding ability guaranteed my boot became wedged firmly in the door of Sydney racing. And the winners just kept on coming.

Sloane arrived and we set up house in a unit at Kensington just a short step from Randwick racecourse. The pain of my ugly departure from Brisbane started to recede, replaced by the conviction that the interstate switch had been a good move. Once again the cat had leaped from a great height and managed to land on his feet.

It wasn't just luck. I had arrived in Sydney with an absolute conviction to give it a red-hot go. I wasn't going home with my tail between legs. By early 1994 I was getting into the groove of riding in Sydney and beyond, and was prepared to travel far and wide to improve my experience and push my credentials. I criss-crossed the map of New South Wales – Gosford, Wyong, Kembla Grange, Hawkesbury, Broadmeadow, Forbes, Warren, Orange and Bathurst, plus some places I had never heard of before – willing to ride anywhere and everywhere. Have saddle, will travel might have been my calling card.

As a bright-eyed kid from the Gold Coast I was surprised and thrilled when the great Bart Cummings put me on almost straightaway to ride work. In no time I was riding winners for him. As a young bloke growing up in the world of horseflesh, the man they called the 'Cups King' was one of the legends of the game – and was a remote and distant presence. Meeting him was a great honour. Being put in charge of some of his horses on race day almost exceeded my wildest dreams. Our relationship got off on the right foot from day one and has endured in that way until this day.

Around horses Bart is all business, that sharp eye forever watching, assessing, picking out small details invisible to the rest. It is hard to believe there was ever a better judge of horseflesh. If you have watched him over the years you may have picked up on the fact that his sense of humour is just as sharp. I soon learned that he was a master of one-liners, a genuinely funny man with a humorous observation on just about everything.

Another turf legend I would get to know in those early days in Sydney was Jack Denham. One of the greatest misconceptions about the Australian racing scene surrounds him. The great old trainer has a reputation for being impervious as stone. If you follow the media line, it would be easier getting a comment out of an Easter Island statue than anything out of Jack Denham. So ingrained was this thinking that a generation of reporters sought easier marks rather than approaching the flint-eyed old mentor for a quote. That impression couldn't be further from the truth. From the first time I met him, Jack was always up for chat, especially with people whose company he enjoyed. Luckily, I have been one of them. Our relationship grew stronger much later in my career when I became associated with Jack's horse Eremein. Although there was almost 50 years age difference between jockey and trainer, I suspected that Jack's time as a jockey before he took out his training licence created a bit of a bond with those who rode for him. A member of a Sydney training dynasty, for six successive years he was runner-up to TJ Smith for the Sydney trainers' premiership table before breaking through to collect the title in 1990–91 and 1992–93.

On the metropolitan tracks I was in the company of great riders. Jim Cassidy, Mick Dittman, Kevin Moses, Shane Dye and Darren Beadman were masters of their craft and I wasn't in their class. Not yet. It was a lively world peopled by savvy individuals all making a living of sorts in and around Sydney thoroughbred racing.

Everything was on a larger scale in Sydney. At track work each day you would be dealing with millions of dollars worth of horseflesh. That sort of responsibility might make some riders nervous but it never bothered me. Instead, the attraction of being on great horses was way too big an opportunity to succumb to stage fright. Today, it's quite a thrill getting on these beautiful colts knowing that you can help them produce a performance which will make their reputation as stud prospects from which they could turn out million-dollar babies and, down the track, you might be riding them too. You can help build a dynasty.

It follows that those with enough cash to burn will invest in the glamorous world of thoroughbred ownership and buy some of those talented offspring. The Sydney that I landed in back in 1994 was the city of the mega-rich Ingham Brothers, the Packers, John Singleton, Gerry Harvey and a host of glittering names and syndicates eager to get the ultimate bang for their buck. Along for the ride were an army of syndicate members happy to pool their cash and purchase a share in a racehorse. It was a world of large personalities, big money and superstar trainers. I found it irresistible.

There are two great competitions among jockeys. One takes place out on the track. The other is less obvious but equally cut-throat. It is the battle to get yourself on the best horse. As a new face in Sydney I was a long way off the pace in this second contest. Sure, plenty of rides were coming my way but the best ones were going to blokes who had been riding in Sydney longer and had better career records, especially in the race that counted – the Group 1 events.

Fairly early in the piece, I became associated with the stable of Gai Waterhouse who had taken over the running of the famous Tulloch Lodge from her dad TJ Smith. Shane Dye was the stable's number one rider and at best I was number two. That meant he would usually be on the race favourite and I would be on the 10–1 pop. There was no point complaining about the situation because racing is driven by results and, at that point, I didn't even have a Group 1 victory to my name, whereas Shane was at the very pinnacle of the business.

It occurred to me that until I graduated to the ranks of riders with Group 1 victories under their belts, I would remain second-best, a talented journeyman who never cracked the big time. As the bloke who rarely jumped up on the race favourite, especially when the big events came around, I knew that my first Group 1 win would have to come against the odds.

His name was Telesto and, in so many ways, the odds were definitely against him. He was a big colt with a turn of speed that would have the clockers at track work shaking their timepieces to see if they were working properly. He was that fast. But come race day, that awesome speed was often undone by his quirky personality. Named after the 10th of Jupiter's moons, Telesto set me a real challenge: how to get this celestial body orbiting a racetrack at a speed that suited me rather than him?

The fact that Shane Dye had ridden the colt and passed him on for a more tractable mount just about said it all. Telesto was an enigma. I had ridden him in track work and he was fine. But, come race day, he would miss the jump every time. Giving the field a six-length start at the barrier is the sort of stunt that has punters tearing up their betting slips in frustration and sending trainers old before their time. If you shook him up to recover ground, he would get his back up and simply refuse to race. The only strategy that seemed to work was to sit patiently and wait until he tacked on to the rear of the field. Once he made contact, he could run the final 600 metres in an astonishing 33.5 seconds. It was a nerve-racking ride but it was the only way he could race. Once you worked Telesto out and went with him rather than against him, you prayed that his blinding speed would have you thereabouts when the finish post flashed by. If you didn't know better, you would swear he was doing it on purpose. 'I can give them a six-length start and still beat them,' he seemed to be saying, 'provided you let me run the race that suits me.'

With Shane declining the ride, I was on Telesto for the 1994 Group 1 Chipping Norton Stakes at Warwick Farm. By then I had my strategy worked out. Whatever happened at the start, I was determined to be patient and let him work his way back into the race.

The gates flew open and Telesto did his best imitation of one of those equestrian statues you see in city squares. He didn't move. By the time he got going the field was gone. Remember, this is a Group 1 event, so giving a class field a six-length start just about defies every theory of racing logic. 'Just be patient,' I kept saying to myself. True to his form, at the half mile we were back in contact with the field. But the big question left to be answered was after recovering all that ground, how much did he have left in the tank? We were about to find out. At the 600-metre mark I lit him up and he went *wump*! His turn of speed had to be experienced to be believed. I was riding an equine rocket! Gone was the difficult horse with the contrary ways. Instead, underneath me was a pure racing machine. Like a supercharged dragster, Telesto flattened out in a ground-swallowing surge. In the classic manner of thoroughbred colts, he clearly wanted to charge to the front of the herd and show them who was boss. In that mood, Telesto simply swept by a field of classy gallopers, all of which had enjoyed easier runs. His astounding sprint carried us all the way to the post and a one time Queensland bush jockey all the way to his first Group 1 victory. My wait was over.

6

A lucky break

My second Group 1 success came in the autumn of 1995. The Chipping Norton had broken the duck, but the follow-up victory was in another realm altogether. The story of how I wound up riding the winner of the world's richest race for two-year-olds just about sums up the entire racing industry but, more especially, my uncanny knack of landing on my feet.

Getting fit and healthy for that autumn carnival had been quite a battle. It was a fight I very nearly lost. Six weeks before I was all set to ride a Gai Waterhouse odds-on chance in the Queanbeyan Cup. In the second race of the meeting I was riding a mount for Canberra trainer Frank Cleary when the runners struck trouble immediately in front of me. I could see it coming but there was no way to avoid it as my mount came down in a multi-horse chain reaction. I hit the turf, bounced, rolled and slid. As soon as I came to a stop, I sprang to my feet, shocked and not a little relieved to discover that I was relatively unhurt. Nearby, a horse was on its side trying to get up. The vet would later have to put it down. I ran to one of the stricken jockeys. It was Roley Saxton and by the angle his limb was pointing, it looked like he had broken a leg. Seeing me on my feet, he tried to get up. I grabbed hold of him and laid him back down on his stomach.

'What have I done?' he was asking. 'What have I done?'

He was in shock.

'I think you've broken your leg,' I told him.

A red-hot alarm seemed to be going off in my wrist, but compared with Roley's plight the throbbing pain was no big deal. When the ambulance had cleared the wounded from the battlefield, the stewards asked after my health. I told them I was fine then went straight to Frank Cleary and had him bind my forearm as tight as possible with strips of elastoplast. Bung wrist or not, I had an odds-on pop to ride in the Cup.

For almost the entire duration, the ride went to plan. We jumped and I let him relax just behind the leaders. Everything was looking fine. We hit the front a fair way from home, which would not have been a problem normally but for the fact that this particular mount had a knack of being a bit lazy and forgetting that he was in a race. About a hundred metres out I could feel the runners coming from behind so I gave him a couple of quick ones with the whip. Remember that old saying parents or teachers would use when they were about to give you a whack: 'This is going to hurt me a lot more than it will hurt you'? In this case, it was absolutely true. The persuader might have put my mount's mind back on the job but the shock of using my damaged wrist sent a current of pure agony coursing through my body.

We won, but I don't even remember passing the post. My head was swimming in a sea of pain. Thankfully, the clerk of the course picked us up and got us back to the saddling enclosure where I promptly passed out. The next thing I remember was waking up in Queanbeyan Hospital with my arm in a cast. My chances for the rich races in autumn were not looking too flash.

Back in Sydney an operation pinned the broken scaphoid bone. I rested the injured arm and, a bundle of pure impatience, counted down the weeks. Would there be enough time for the injury to heal? A fortnight before the autumn carnival I was back riding with a brace on my arm.

Of all the Group 1 trophies in Australia, there is a handful truly coveted by owners, trainers and jockeys. The Melbourne Cup is the biggest prize of all. The Cox Plate is an absolute gem because it represents the weight-for-age championship of Australasia. And somewhere right up there in that top bracket sits the race for the youngsters – the Golden Slipper for two-year-olds, which is raced each autumn at Rosehill Gardens in Sydney. The idea of a race for two-year-olds at special weights was conceived by Sydney Turf Club committee member George Ryder. Colts were to carry 54 kilograms and fillies 51. There were 11 starters in the first Slipper field of 1957 when the brilliant colt Todman showed his class. Since then the race has been won by some of the absolute champions of the Australasian turf including Baguette, Vain, Luskin Star, Marscay and Marauding.

Slipper day is an occasion keenly anticipated by the industry and public alike; a day that fills Rosehill to the rafters and introduces gallopers destined to become legends of the turf and breeding industries. The raw age of the field means it is ripe with uncertainty. Odds-on favourites can be easily rolled by long shots that might go on to greatness or sample barely a few moments of turf fame. The combination is compelling: a huge prize purse, a short distance of 1200 metres and a large field of inexperienced colts and fillies makes for inspired and sometimes downright desperate tactics out there on the track.

As if this plot wasn't gripping enough, into the classic of 1995 the fates tipped a few more dramatic elements. When you put them altogether, it made for one of the most unforgettable Slippers of all.

The backdrop to the yarn started to take shape in 1994 when Sydney police had secretly tapped the phones of some individuals thought to be involved in drug trafficking. Word reached the ears of the Australian Jockey Club's chief steward John Schreck that some licensed racing people, including jockeys, had been mentioned on the tapes.

Early on the day before the running of the 1995 Slipper, the chief steward received transcripts of the tapes. On the same morning, the story broke in the Sydney press. The AJC wasted no time, immediately kicking off the enquiries and calling for questioning any licensed individual whose name was mentioned on the tapes. Glen Boss was just one of many that appeared in the transcripts. I made myself available for questioning but in the short time I appeared before the panel it was quite clear that I didn't know any of the people behind the voices on the tapes and had no reason to feel incriminated. It was a revolving door as many of the better known jockeys of the day came and went.

One who didn't was Jimmy Cassidy. On legal advice, Jim declined to appear and was immediately disqualified for six months for refusing to attend an inquiry. With the Slipper just a day away and Jimmy due to ride a smart Lee Freedman-trained colt called Flying Spur, he appealed and applied for a stay of proceedings which was refused by the AJC committee.

The so-called Jockey Tapes were the least of my worries. I had been booked for a ride on a smart filly owned by the advertising tycoon and irrepressible punter John Singleton but she had broken down on the Tuesday. I was devastated. With just a few days to go, I was left high and dry without a ride in one of the greatest races of the year.

Then, at midday on the Friday, word broke that Jimmy had been disqualified. Janelle Freedman was in charge of bookings for the stable and she moved swiftly, ringing the Sydney Turf Club to find out who was without a ride in the Slipper. The answer came straight back: Glen Boss.

Janelle immediately rang my agent Michael O'Brien and the booking was made. There was high excitement in the Boss household. I was on a good one in one of racing's best events and a heavily pregnant Sloane was very close to welcoming our first-born into the world.

In my quest for improvement I had become a fastidious researcher of horseflesh – ploughing through the breeding form in barrier trials and listening closely when the experts spoke. I had studied the two-year-old contenders for the season. Flying Spur had been bred by Arrowfield Stud. At the Australian Easter Yearling Sales, Arrowfield managing director John Messara was less than impressed by a top bid of $160,000 so he brought him back. Flying Spur was considered a good horse who had shown a glimpse of his ability with a second in the Blue Diamond Stakes at Caulfield. But he was a colt in the true sense of the word; a young bloke with a mind of his own who could behave like a champion one day and a goat the next. Frustrated, the Freedmans had informed John Messara that they would probably put him out to paddock and give the Slipper a miss. In fact, they were of a mind to curb Flying Spur's coltish ways with the unkindest cut of all. Messara famously decreed that there was more chance of Lee being cut than Flying Spur and it was just as well because the stallion went on to become a great success at stud.

However, the master trainer who had prepared the previous two Slipper winners obviously hadn't given up. In the lead up he brought Flying Spur from the paddock to Randwick and kept him in work mindful that, if the mood took him, the colt could deliver on the day. With the Freedmans' other leading prospect, Gold Ace, sidelined with chips to his knees, the stable was banking on the wayward colt stepping up to the mark.

Flying Spur was at odds of 25–1 but people in the business knew he was a good chance. I'll never forget Lee's summation: 'He's got so much ability and so much potential. But he's a colt with a mind of his own. He'll either win it or run last.'

Race day was the first time I'd ever been on Flying Spur but straightaway I knew he was something else. You could feel the energy coursing up through him. He was like a bomb about to go off. On the way to the barrier, Gavin Eades, one of the best riders of the time, was cantering up behind me and I was so excited I turned to him and declared: 'This horse is gunna win!'

And win he did. I've always prided myself on my ability to get horses to settle into a race and Flying Spur proved no exception. Whatever his reputation had been for obstinacy and strong-mindedness, we were a perfect partnership that day. He jumped superbly from the inside and settled well. In running, he felt beautiful underneath me. He was travelling sweet at the turn as I started to work him into the race. My plan had been to stick close to the race favourites Octagonal and Strategic but abandoned that plan after noting they were trapped wide. Instead, I opted for the shortest way home knowing the challenges would be coming down the outside. The biggest threat would be in the form of the magnificent black colt Octagonal. As Flying Spur weaved his way through close to the rail, I could just see Occy out of the corner of my eye making his charge out wide. We had a break but would still need everything going our way to hold off the horse destined to become the best of his generation. The gods must have been smiling on me that day because the vital split came at exactly the right time and I squeezed Flying Spur through the gap as the post loomed. Occy was finishing like a dark avalanche down the outside but the line was too close. A lunge and it was done.

We had won by a neck with the filly Millrich a length back in third place. By hugging the rail and taking the shortest way home, the 25–1 pop had aced the favourites. The Slipper was ours. Flashing past the post my instinct was to stand straight up in the irons and celebrate like the winning scorer on grand final day. 'I've won,' I screamed. 'I've won!'

John Schreck had had a busy week and he didn't need another suspension on his hands. Instead, he handed out a stern warning on the folly of premature celebrations. I was lucky. The winning margin was so narrow that any slip could have cost us the race on the line. If I had blown it then, I would have been run out of town all the way back to Gympie.

The enormity of the occasion hit me on the way back and I shed a few tears. The crowd reception was like nothing I had ever encountered. Back in the mounting yard, it was sheer pandemonium. Sloane was beside herself. We had made quite a journey together. The Freedman clan realised they had pulled off an incredible coup as did John Messara and the Arrowfield connections. And, after the dramatic events leading up to the race, the media crush was unbelievable.

The celebrations continued after the trophy presentation and I was still buzzing as I headed out to the barrier on what proved to be my consecutive winner of the day.

As for Flying Spur, all faith in the one-time wayward colt was justified. As a three-year-old he would go on to win the Australian Guineas, the AJC All-Aged Stakes and the STC Peter Pan Stakes. He was placed at Group 1 level on seven occasions before retiring to a grand stud career at Arrowfield in the Hunter Valley.

LEE FREEDMAN: 'Flying Spur eventually developed into a very manageable horse but, as a two-year-old, he was really difficult. So, it was a massive bonus to win such a big race early in his career. As for gelding him, that would have been the absolute last resort. It was suggested more as a joke.'

That day was another big turning point in my career. Yes, winning the Chipping Norton had been important, but the Slipper victory and the against-the-odds way in which it had been achieved took me to another place. I had arrived in Sydney as an energetic if ill-disciplined jockey who would do whatever was required to win a race. But now, that win-at-all-costs attitude had been tempered by a dash of maturity and finesse.

But I was still young and green enough to revel in the victory. This was the dream coming true. As a raw apprentice, I had watched and re-watched my tape of the great Manikato winning the 1978 Slipper. Now, I had managed to ride all the way from the rough tracks of country Queensland to the lush surrounds of Rosehill to write my own name in the tale of the great race.

The adrenalin was still running at a million volts as we stepped out to party that night. If you hooked me up to a set of jumper leads I could have lit up a city. Sometimes I wish I could bottle that sensation and hand it out for others to sample to show just what it feels like to back yourself and ride a winner in a Golden Slipper, Cox Plate or Melbourne Cup. There is nothing like it. Your entire being goes into hyper-drive and your emotions just let go. In the wee small hours, after the partying was done, I was still too wired to go home as we sat sipping coffee in Double Bay. I wanted the feeling to last and last.

What makes those big races so exceptional is that you appreciate just how much goes in to making it happen and how easily miserable fortune can bring it all undone. The Freedmans had walked a hard road to bring Flying Spur to hand on the day. Jimmy Cassidy missed out and his disappointment would have been boundless. And so would have mine if I hadn't scored a ride in the Slipper.

When you tally them up, it took a string of minor miracles and strange events to get me and Flying Spur to the barrier on Slipper day. That's the nature of the game. That's why, when you win a big one, you never take it for granted. I had won my first truly major Group 1 event. Like an addict, I hungered for more.

7

So near . . . and yet so far

With that Slipper victory came a new sense of belonging. My winning bonus helped us put down a deposit on a new home in the seaside suburb of Malabar. But the event that truly indicated we had put down meaningful roots in Australia's largest city was the arrival of our first born, a son we called Tayte. Sloane and I had lobbed in the big smoke as a couple and now we were a family of three. We had created something new and wonderful. Five years later Tayte would have a little sister, Carter. For now, we felt, we truly belonged in Sydney Town.

Being accepted by my fellow jockeys also helped. At first, I realised that my modest riding record was nothing alongside the multiple Group successes of the established Sydney stars. But my work ethic and growing reputation wasn't going unnoticed.

I didn't want to be a mediocre rider. For company and the chance to learn the tricks of the trade, I spent plenty of my spare time with another former Queenslander, Mick Dittman, and the ex-Kiwi Shane Dye. Both were at the absolute top of their craft and the more time I could spend in their company the better the chance of picking up pearls of wisdom.

Another rider who was a terrific influence at the time was Greg Hall. In fact, we became great mates. Whereas I was probably wound up a bit tight and never satisfied with myself, Greg was a knockabout larrikin, a bloke at peace with life, the world and himself. He struck me as a real character and terrific fun to be around. Like me, he used to get into the odd bit of trouble with race stewards. But, in a big race on the right mount, he wouldn't get beat. In the jockeys' room on a Melbourne Cup or Cox Plate day he would be laughing it up, then he'd go out and do the job, return to the room and still be telling jokes. Even at the barrier he'd be cracking lines about how you robbed him at golf the previous day. No matter how strained the occasion, he would always have a ready joke. It's hard to believe that such a relaxed individual could exist in such an ultra-competitive environment. But don't be fooled. When it came to getting the job done, there were few better. Once the gates flew open, he was all business. Even good jockeys can slaughter a race favourite, but he was like a computer in coming up with the right answer every time. By comparison, I was too intense for my own good. On meeting and getting to know Greg, I grew to appreciate how he had it all in proportion. I liked to think that some of his relaxed ways had started to rub off on me. Mind you, I was still way too tense, angry and uptight about my high expectations and per-ceived failures. But getting to know Greg Hall was a positive start. I loved his attitude and he influenced me to the point whereby I can see a bit of him in me today.

So many of today's young jockeys only know about TJ Smith by reputation. My arrival in Sydney coincided with his final few years as a trainer so I was lucky enough to ride for the man who dominated Australian racing for decades. He put me on plenty of horses and I managed to ride my share of Group winners for him.

Part of the legend was the toughness of his upbringing as a boy in rural New South Wales. He retained that tough edge all his life. Boy, was he hard! He was hard on his staff and hard on his riders, but he was scrupulously fair. He was a sticker and I enjoyed his company immensely.

One of his greatest joys was to sit around after track work and talk. He always had time for young people. I took the time to read his biography and marvel at the way he built a great racing empire from scratch. His eye for detail extended to every part of his business and he missed nothing. He made sure he put his poverty-stricken origins well behind him by dressing immaculately every time he stepped out the door and he carried himself so well.

They say that putting yourself next to winners is one of the best ways to learn. In those early days in Sydney I noted what time TJ Smith arrived for track work at Randwick and exactly where he would park his car. Australia's greatest-ever trainer was meant to be enjoying his retirement years but obviously finding old habits hard to break, he still turned up at 4 am for track work. I made a point of arriving just a minute or two before and would be waiting for him so that we could walk across the tracks together to the timing hut in the infield. I'd like to think that he appreciated the company because, at that stage of his life, TJ wasn't too spry and his sight and hearing weren't too flash. There are some seriously quick racehorses working out there in the dark and getting across half-a-dozen courses means you better have your wits about you.

Tommy Smith – what a legend. He always had time for a chat about racing or his life, which pretty much were one and the same thing. This was the man who won 33 consecutive Sydney training premierships and retired with a total of 34; a bloke who had grown up in the bush working hard from the age of seven until his uncanny ability to assess and prepare thoroughbreds changed his life and, eventually, the shape of Australian racing. Nobody could match Tommy's knack for spotting a horse and working out whether it had the ability to win a race for him. He fed his horses the best, worked them harder than other trainers and turned them out with a 'bone and muscle' look that became the trademark of TJ Smith gallopers. With champions like Kingston Town, Gunsynd, Redcraze, Imagele, Red Anchor and Bounding Away, he saddled up 279 Group 1 winners. His Tulloch Lodge head-quarters, named after the most famous of all Smith gallopers, became the greatest racing dynasty in the land, the control of which would eventually be handed on to his daughter Gai Waterhouse in the early 1990s. Tommy would pass away in 1998 aged 82 but not before seeing Gai collect her first trainer's premiership the previous year. It must give TJ great delight, watching from the stand up there in the great beyond, to note that Gai has kept the spirit burning at Tulloch Lodge.

In the gloom of those Randwick mornings I was mindful of being in the presence of racing greatness as the old trainer and the kid from Queensland made their way through the early mist across the course proper. His faculties might have been failing but his uncanny instinct for horseflesh was as sharp as ever. When a good one, especially a Group horse, would come steaming like a train out of the dark, Tommy would squeeze my arm and gesture with his walking cane: 'What's that one son, what's that one?'

'Ah, that's Saintly,' or 'That's March Hare, Mr Smith,' I would say.

As ever, he would have picked out a good one.

'I'll see if I can buy it,' he would declare.

And that's what Tommy Smith did better than anybody – acquired horses with potential and turned them into goldmines. When Sloane and I purchased our house in Malabar, Tommy told me he had once owned a large slab of the suburb. He had bought the land years before, when it was a rundown area, had waited for the demand for coastal real estate to go through the roof, and then sold it. He was a self-made multimillionaire and, obviously, one of the canniest blokes racing had every known.

As TJ Smith understood, the greatest gift in the racing game is to be able to spot a good horse before your rivals do. For a jockey it is crucial. It means you're on a winner and your rivals are somewhere down the track. If you become associated with a quality galloper early in its career and you do the right thing by it and the connections, chances are you will get to stick with it. So, for trainers, owners, punters and eventually jockeys, right from the time the yearlings step into the sales ring, the contest is on to spot the ones with the right bloodlines, confirmation and temperament to develop into winners. My working day consists of two prime chores: riding and researching horses.

As the hired gun engaged to ride a thoroughbred, a jockey should know as soon as he gets up on a horse if it has that special ingredient. I don't know exactly how to describe it. In some ways, it's more of a feeling, a sensation given off by the animal. Some people say that a great galloping action is a sure sign. But I've been on average horses that have had great actions. An action might look good but doesn't necessarily denote speed. Galloping is usually a sound test because that's when you find out if they have genuine speed. As soon as they gallop you know if they are quick or not. Three-quarter pace is standard practice in track work and it will tell you if a horse has the potential to go fast. One horse's three-quarter pace might be 15 seconds to the furlong (just over 200 metres) while another might be 13 but seemingly doing it much easier. You bring him back and the trainer will ask: 'Do you know how fast you were going? You were doing 13 and a half to the furlong!'

Meanwhile, the horse has pulled up easy, not blowing like a set of bellows, but breathing comfortably. That backs up the initial impression you got when first jumping up on to him: this is a good horse. Of course, going fast in training doesn't necessarily relate to winning on race day. But it is a start.

In so many ways I had taken to life in Sydney like a thirsty bloke to a cold beer. But, as comfortable as I felt in the harbour city, I was still a Queenslander at heart and a great supporter of all things from the Sunshine state. Sydney may have been the birthplace of rugby league in Australia, but my allegiances would always rest with two great sides north of the Tweed River – the Brisbane Broncos and the Queensland State of Origin team. Being a fella who gave away a fair bit of size as a junior footballer, I always identified with the smaller blokes.

And, pound for pound, the best of them all was the number seven for the Broncos, Queensland and Australia, Allan Langer.

Alfie, as his friends called him, never had any trouble darting through the best rugby league defences but he didn't need those nimble feet to step inside my close circle of friends. There was nothing auspicious about our first contact – in fact, I can't even remember it. We were just two sports entities on the Brisbane – Gold Coast scene who would have come in contact at a corporate function or sponsors day and started chatting.

Like most fans, I was in awe of his skill and courage. As a card-carrying member of the little bloke's brigade, I certainly identified with him. We kept bumping into each other at the football, golf days and corporate functions and soon became great mates.

Any competitive athlete can learn by watching an Alfie Langer. As a little bloke in a tough game, he had courage to burn. He combined a great heart with a tremendous football brain that allowed him to read the opposition and work out how he was going to take them apart. Unpredictable, he could turn a game in the blink of an eye.

Off the field, Alfie is modest and honest as the day is long. He lives his life by a code of honesty. That said, he enjoys a beer, a bet and rugby league. Having watched his career and appreciated him from afar as a superstar of the game, I thought he would be remote, a bit difficult to get to know. Instead, he was the exact opposite and he surrounded himself with people who were every bit as easygoing. He never needed celebrity status, in fact, he was a bit embarrassed by it, but he would never let anyone down or disappoint his legion of fans.

The night before Sloane and I were married in Port Douglas, we had a night out on the town with our friends. Halfway through proceedings, we noticed we had lost Alf. Eventually, we found him in a nearby pub with a pen in one hand, a pile of beer coasters for signing stacked up in front of him and a queue of admirers waiting their turn for an autograph. Was Alf put out? Not likely; he was laughing, cracking jokes and posing for photos with the fans. He is the sort of bloke who would make time for anyone.

In many ways he is the complete larrikin – always smiling, happy and up for a joke. I can recall seeing him dirty on himself or the opposite team, but I've never seen him angry. He is too busy enjoying life. That personality makes people gravitate to him. Alfie might be small in stature but, in so many other ways, he is larger than life.

If I have something to get off my chest, I know I can confide in Alfie.

When he was playing in England I kept in constant contact with him, suspecting that he might be missing home and his mates. I'd grown to understand that Alf is never happier than when he is surrounded by friends and he is helping brighten up their lives. What they give to him and he gives back in return defies description. While the mateship and bonding element is strong in Australian clubs, especially in the Broncos' team of that era, it is not necessarily so evident in England. Alf was doing his bit on the playing field but definitely missing the company and camaraderie off it. So, he and I burned the phone lines between Australia and England.

In retirement from football he has been a real success story as a family man and with his business interests in the restaurant game. It's a privilege to call him a mate.

With me in Sydney and friends like Alf in Brisbane, I have always felt connected in the best way to my home state.

After the euphoria of the autumn of 1995, I was on serious alert for top quality horseflesh capable of adding to my meagre tally of two Group 1 victories. Luckily, winning the Slipper was worth a million dollars in publicity for a jockey on the way up. My phone line was buzzing with offers from owners and trainers willing to put me on quality horses.

The Flight Stakes at Randwick is named after a champion mare who won a string of Group 1 races, including the Cox Plate twice. It's restricted to three-year-old fillies and covers a journey of 1600 metres.

One of the best of her year was a beautiful filly sired by the champion galloper Marauding. Pontal Lass was trained by Clarry Connors and I was more than pleased to be on her in the Flight. She became one of four Group 1 winners I managed to ride in season 1995–96.

Among the high points of the season was riding the first Group 1 winner for trainer Rod Craig on his brilliant chestnut colt Intergaze in the Champagne Stakes at Randwick. But, from a personal career viewpoint, the two most important wins were on Electronic and Sprint By because both were campaigned by the trainer soon to be dubbed 'Mrs Racing' – Gai Waterhouse. To be riding and winning big races for Gai was, arguably, the most tangible sign that I had carved myself a viable place in Sydney racing.

When Gai took over the running of the racing business created by her father TJ Smith, Shane Dye was her number one rider, but I soon became the stable number two. Previously I have spoken about the work ethic of horse people, the business of rising early when most of the world is fast asleep and getting a solid day's work done before the rest has finished breakfast. Among the legion of hard workers I have met in this game, nobody can touch Gai Waterhouse. When it comes to putting in the hours of slog attending to the thousands of chores and daily issues that constitute running a major stable, she is the absolute gold medallist. She rises early, works hard all day and brings with it a level of enthusiasm that leaves mere mortals exhausted in her wake. I don't know when she finds time to sleep. I can recollect messaging her at 2.30 am only to have her call me straight back.

Not only did Gai take up where her dad had left off, she brought a new level of customer focus to the business. At Tulloch Lodge it became all about the owners, the people whose bucks bought and fed the horses and underpinned the business. She opened up the Lodge in a way that gave the owners insight and access, plus a clearer understanding of what was involved in preparing a racehorse. Her philosophy demanded staff adhere to the owners' needs. In so doing, she brought a whole new approach to the game which has since been adopted by other trainers.

In the course of time, I would ride less and less for Gai. Call it a battle of wills if you like. As boss of a big stable she wanted to exercise a certain control over the riding ranks by having a good bank of jockeys on call. That would be okay if the rider was getting a full commitment from her stable. But, with the volume of jockeys she had on her list, the risk was that you became just one of the numbers. That system doesn't fit with me. It's not my style. I prefer to freelance. We agreed to butt heads on that issue, but it didn't diminish my respect for this hard-working, brilliant horsewoman. Since acquiring her licence, the immaculately dressed, larger-than-life personality has constantly put racing on the front page and given it a profile that TJ might have only dreamed about. In my initial seasons in Sydney, being associated with her stable was an honour and a fabulous opportunity.

The Metropolitan Handicap was first run back in 1863 and has long featured as one of the nation's major staying events. The big Randwick race had a special place in the training career of Gai because it gave the daughter of TJ Smith her first Group 1 win when Mick Dittman rode Te Akau Nick to victory in 1992. Three years later she was looking for her second Metrop when she saddled up another New Zealand-bred stayer by the name of Electronic. It was gratifying to be a part of that successful campaign. Like Mick Dittman, I was the next Brisbane jockey to have headed south to win a Metrop with Gai.

During my first few months in Sydney, what seemed like another routine afternoon at Hawkesbury races had been transformed by a smart gelding called Sprint By. It was only a maiden win but on returning to the weigh scale I remarked that the galloper – by the New Zealand sire Kaapstaad out of the American dam Brookes Cross – just might win a big race one day. In fact, my words to Gai were: 'This one is gunna win a Doncaster!'

He was certainly capable of winning a major event but while preparing for the Doncaster he copped a setback when he tore a hoof. Word got around that he was unsound and one trainer even proposed that Sprint By be subject to a veterinary inspection. The injury caused him to miss a bit of work but I knew him inside out and was confident he would be 100 per cent on the day. As extra insurance, Gai had special shoes fitted to protect the sensitive spot.

The Randwick course is a tough haul, especially when the

opposition is provided by Group 1 gallopers prepared to perfection to take out the rich prize money on offer. I'll admit, we
had some luck, but we also made our own. Jumping from a
wide barrier I knew where we wanted to be – in the one-one
position – one out from the rail and one back from the lead.
And that's exactly where we were when they settled down. My
strategy was to avoid getting trapped when those behind us
started making their runs. I knew we needed to get out and
make our run at exactly the right time. As they say, timing is
everything. Getting to the front too soon would have been
disastrous and getting there too late would have cost us our
chance. We had to be in control of our own destiny. The race
strategy worked perfectly with absolutely nothing to spare.
A half-head was the winning margin over second-placed
Danasinga, with stablemate Juggler back in third position.
Together Sprint By and I won at Gosford, Canterbury and
Randwick. With the exception of missing two starts while
serving a suspension, I rode Sprint By for his entire career.

The Melbourne spring carnival beckoned and the prospect
of adding to my reputation with a first Group 1 win in that city
was extremely enticing. Gai sent the team south with Shane
Dye and yours truly assigned to look after the bulk of track
work and race riding. Melbourne proved a tougher nut to crack
than I could have imagined. I appeared in the winner's circle
on just two occasions while Shane had a bountiful carnival,
especially when aboard the stable star Nothin' Leica Dane in
the Norman Robinson Stakes and the Victoria Derby. For the
boy from Caboolture, it was a dry old spring and proved that
he was still a long way short of where he wanted to be.

8

Up and down

In 1997 the first opportunity for me to ride in Hong Kong presented itself. The former British colony boasts one of the most sophisticated racing scenes in the world, and the Hong Kong Jockey Club has traditionally looked to Australia to recruit racing staff, stewards and executives. Consequently, there is a powerful Australian influence throughout the entire Hong Kong racing scene. For trainers and jockeys, a stint in the gambling-mad metropolis of more than five million people can be extremely lucrative, with the proceeds only second to Japan in international racing.

As it turned out, Hong Kong was indeed a goldmine but more for the lessons it delivered rather than tax-free dollars. It was here, such a long way from home, that I was to receive one of the most valuable lessons of my career, an education that would pay off time and time again.

The truth was, I was struggling and Hong Kong is not a

good place to be when you are down on your luck, confidence and form. It was the year the one-time jewel in the British colonial crown was to be handed over to Chinese rule. It was a time of excitement, speculation and real uncertainty. But this new arrival was hardly buzzing with anticipation, let alone triumph.

If I had thought the scramble among jockeys for rides back home was a bunfight, this new environment delivered a shock. In Hong Kong, the rivalry among jockeys was absolutely cut-throat, ruthless in the extreme. There was no trick that some jockeys wouldn't use to get you off a horse that they wanted to ride. On one occasion, a jockey who wanted to get on the horse I was due to ride rang the trainer and told him I had taken another ride. It was an outright lie. It was a desperate, un-official business with its prime purpose to preserve the status quo for certain jockeys by shutting out any newcomers. In so many ways I was still a country boy from Queensland who imagined that he had picked up some street wisdom along the way. But Hong Kong was in an entirely different league. I was a babe amid the tower blokes of an ultra-competitive city.

It's rare in such a dog-eat-dog environment that somebody might be aware of what you are going through and offers a hand. Tony Cruz was destined to become the city's leading trainer in his own right with a string of brilliant horses, includ-ing the champion Silent Witness, in his stable. But back in '97 he was an assistant trainer, having recently hung up his saddle after a stellar international riding career. He was one of those jockeys who could make riding a horse look like poetry. Noting that I was down on form and confidence, it was Tony who imparted the wisdom and technique of 'toe-in'.

The first time I had noticed the toe-in style was while watching videos of international races, notably from Europe and the United States. I had been particularly impressed by how the Americans could get low but still get their weight forward. The natural instinct for anybody jumping up on a horse is to set the stirrup in the middle of the arch of the foot. It seems a comfortable fit and provides grip. But those videos had shown me that the best jockeys were using a different technique. Instead of the iron being set back under the arch, it was positioned under the very toes of the rider. Hence toe-in. Keen to learn more, I approached Tony Cruz.

Tony talked about the centre of balance up through the legs to the withers – that high point up behind the horse's neck. The aim, he said, was to get the rider's centre of balance to coincide with that. I was struggling with the concept until he put me on a horse and demonstrated exactly what he meant. It clicked right away and felt brilliant. However, putting it into effect would take a deal of perseverance. Old habits die hard. But, eventually, I would get it nailed and become an advocate for the toe-in style to any young riders who sought my advice. The toe-in style actually means you are riding 'longer'. By taking the weight on your toes instead of your arch, the length of the foot adds to your height in the saddle. Therefore, you can set the irons shorter to compensate.

Another compelling reason for riding toe-in is that it is part insurance against a jockey's greatest fear: the risk of getting hooked up and dragged. If something goes wrong in a race, and a jockey is unseated from his mount, a toe-in rider has less chance of having his foot trapped in the stirrup, which is the predicament we know as 'getting hooked up'.

As a kid riding in Brisbane, I was cruising to the line on a certain winner when it suddenly shied. I was pitched sideways off the horse but managed to hold on to its neck. The best strategy might have been to abandon ship altogether but to my horror I couldn't free one foot from the iron. I was hooked up. By then I was hanging on under the horse's neck while it was starting to gallop on me. The risk of getting dragged was very real. If my hands slipped from its neck, I would be swinging by one boot under the horse's hooves with the prospect of it literally kicking me to death before it came to a halt. Miraculously, we went across the line with me still gripping its neck like grim death to finish in third place.

It would have been handy to have learned the toe-in lesson earlier, but you are never too old to pick up a new trick. The technique travelled back with me from Hong Kong and since then I have been advocating it to all.

Another valuable message Tony imparted was the wisdom of less is more. Think about it. Next time you are piggybacking a child and they are sitting dead still, feel how much easier it is to carry the weight, to go faster for longer. If the rider is moving around, you are working overtime to keep balance which means you are shedding energy. The theory is exactly the same on a thoroughbred. Sit quiet and still. Concentrate on balance and rhythm. Keep the stick to a minimum.

Of all the elements in the jockey's armoury, the whip is the most easily and uselessly abused. When I think of that image – usually more prevalent in provincial races – of a field of jockeys waving their whip arms like windmills on speed, belting their horses 40 to 50 times all the way down the straight, it makes me angry.

I hate bashing horses because they just curl up underneath you anyway. When they are at their top doing their level best, don't hit them. Sometimes you might give them a tap or two in the straight to encourage them or keep their mind on the job. But the notion that wielding the whip produces speed is just crazy. Instead, the whole idea is to keep them in rhythm so they will run at their best for longer.

Good jockeys realise that they must have respect for the animal. Horses are bred to run and, generally, they are out there doing their best. To flog them means paying them no respect. Some horses will respond to a whopping. But not many. In most cases it is all about encouragement. The Australian racing culture demands that the punters see a horse being ridden to the full extent of its capacity. That will never change. But that can still be achieved in a way that respects the galloper. My style is to hardly ever whack them. I know that there are plenty in the game who will disagree with me. But, as far as I am concerned, it is not just an opinion, I believe it to be a fact. I have tried both methods and know by hard experience what works. As a young jockey I used to bash my rides but, just when you wanted them to be at their fastest, you would feel them curl up underneath you. Why whop them for 200 metres? Commonsense says you want the horses flying over the last 100 metres so you don't want to start whopping them at the top of the straight. Watch the top riders in action, guys like Damien Oliver and Darren Beadman – they use finesse to get the best out of a horse. You don't see them cutting them up at the top of the straight.

It's a fine line between flying and falling off. Good jockeys can make it look effortless. That's the beauty. But when you strip it down to its essentials, riding a thoroughbred at speed seems like a freakish accomplishment. The horse is almost half a tonne of bone and muscle, bred to be a powerful racing machine. But unlike a car or a bike, this 'machine' has a mind and a personality of its own, complete with all the fears and foibles inherent in an intelligent animal. A breaker will carefully school this wild thing to the point whereby it can be ridden, but not by just anybody, only an expert. In bringing the thorough-bred to this stage of its education, it is imperative that a signifi-cant part of its wild spirit be retained. That spirit is the magical ingredient that embodies courage and competitiveness. It's the eternal link to their forebears, wild horses running free long before humans ever thought of throwing a rope around them. It's their spirit that also gives them their sense of independence, defines their personality and, sometimes, makes them unpre-dictable and, occasionally, a little dangerous.

My experience is that if you are cool and calm around horses, they pick up on that and remain calm. Some horses respond to different people. We talk about horses that no adult can possibly get near let alone catch. Next thing, a small child is walking between the animal's legs without spooking it. Horse folk will tell you about animals that have a different respect for different people. It's a vibe and a horse will pick up on it straightaway.

In all my years around horses, the eternal puzzle of what makes them tick has never failed to keep me on my toes. The more you understand a thoroughbred, the better the chance of being able to jump up on his back and forge a winning part-nership. The good ones have that special edge. It is particularly noticeable in the mares. The old Australian expression is 'a bit of mongrel'. You like them to have that bit of 'mongrel', that bit of arrogance and fire, so long as it's channelled in the right direction. In understanding horses, we must appreciate that they are a herding animal. They look to the herd for protection and to run with the mob. I've watched documentaries on wild brumbies and noted the big whaler out the front. He may drop back through the pack but, if there is some threat, he'll charge back to the front and lead them to safety.

A racing thoroughbred must have the best of those twin instincts: an ability to run with the herd but, when asked to, the instinct to get to the front and stamp its leadership qualities on the rest of the mob. Through hundreds of years of breeding, those ingredients have been identified and reproduced to the point where it is fair to say that the modern thoroughbred is born and bred to race. The instinct is so strong. It's like a blue cattle dog pup who has never seen a cow in his life but will go charging around the yard rounding up the chooks. So strong are the instincts that he literally can't help himself from chasing those chickens.

Down through the years the breeding process has made thoroughbreds stronger and faster. The best genes prevail.

Up on to the back of this animal we leg individuals drawn from the lightweight end of the athletic spectrum. Little guys, short in stature but big on nerve and self-belief. Watch them in action. When galloping a racehorse there is barely more than a few centimetres of body and boot in contact at any given time. If a jockey is riding toe-in, this contact is even less. The weight is thrust forward up over the animal's powerful shoulders so that the horse feels he is carrying next to nothing. Big horse, small rider. It is an intriguing partnership. When it works, it is truly a wonder to behold. When it goes wrong, it can be disastrous.

If you enter this relationship for the long haul, you must anticipate a bit of pain. Back in my pony club days, particularly when show jumping, falling off went with the territory. Usually, you bounced to your feet, dusted yourself off and jumped straight back on. At that level, you are gripping with your knees and have plenty of contact with the horse so the rider is not so easy to dislodge. If a horse falls or shies, you usually go with them. The risk of falling off a racing thoroughbred is much greater.

At Terry Chinner's place at Gympie a horse slipped out from under me. I jumped straight to my feet and chased the horse before noticing a persistent pain in my shoulder. I finished up in Nambour Hospital where X-rays revealed a broken collarbone. Maybe if I had given it time to heal properly I wouldn't have been left with a bony bump on the injury site.

As apprentices, nobody ever talked about getting hurt. Was it bravado or a simple realisation that it was no use wasting our breath on discussing the obvious? All of us knew that you must respect the game. None of us could afford to be blasé about it. But sooner or later you are bound to fall. When it happens you are in the lap of the gods, so why worry about it? If a horse breaks down in front of you, if your mount breaks a leg, or if you get caught up in a chain reaction, you are not in control and there is very little you can do except hope that once everything stops, you are still in one piece.

The awful truth is that no matter how hard we try to make racing safe, fatalities do occur. As I said earlier, jockeys rarely talk about the danger. The exception to that rule is when a rider is killed in a race fall. At the next meeting there will be discussions in the jockeys' room and the riders will draw close together and talk about what went wrong. Then we put it out of our minds and get on with the job. You can't go out there on to the track with those negative thoughts in your head. You have to put it behind you. A number of times in my career

I have been involved in a fall and then gone out and won the next race. It's the old story: life isn't so much about what happens to you, but what you choose to do about it. On Melbourne Cup day, 2003, I was involved in a race fall but managed to ride the winner of the next race and then, later on that afternoon, be first past the post in the Cup.

One routine afternoon at Gosford was sorely interrupted when I came off and had the misfortune of being trodden on by another runner. A hoof, with the full weight of a galloping thoroughbred behind it, came squarely down on my thigh. The imprint of the shoe was clearly visible. At first, I was convinced my femur was definitely broken. There was no question of me riding the next race or any more that day. Luckily, there was no break but my thigh was excruciatingly corked. With important barrier trials and track work to be ridden on the Friday morning followed by a Saturday meeting at Randwick, I was determined to get back in the saddle. That night was spent with an ice pack on my thigh. First thing next morning, a hot bath helped loosen it up. The leg was still extremely sore but I wasn't about to tell anybody. I just made some adjustments. I rode longer simply because I couldn't bend my leg enough to fit my foot in the iron. In fact, I couldn't even lift the leg to pull my stocking on. But the main point was that I rode and kept my faith with the owners and trainers who had entrusted me with their horses.

On those occasions it helps to have a medic who understands the athlete's desire to return to the action as soon as possible. As a former first grade rugby league player and later a sports physician with the Australian Rugby League and the Sydney Swans, Dr Nathan Gibbs knew the territory well. Whenever I banged myself up on the job, he would usually get a call.

His phone rang soon after a Chipping Norton Stakes meeting at Warwick Farm where I had been involved in a heavy fall, which knocked me out. Having a headache was one thing, but nothing compared to the awful pain in the rear end. Again, a horse had trodden on me, this time high on the buttock. The legacy was a massive haematoma, an ugly reservoir of congealed blood. Gibbsy produced a needle so big it looked like a cartoon prop. Inserting it in the bruised area, he withdrew a syringe full of black liquid. He repeated the process two more times before the area was completely drained. It left a large indent but I was in no position to complain. While the haematoma was there, I couldn't ride. The indent would eventually go away but one effect of that fall would remain. The impact had pushed a disc in my lower back against the sciatic nerve, creating ongoing pain and problems with the corresponding hamstring muscle. Such injuries are commonplace in racing. In fact, there wouldn't be many jockeys over the age of 25 who aren't managing back, knee or ankle problems.

9

Four screws and a
second chance

Macau, June 2002. When it rains in this part of the world it is like the backside has fallen out of the sky. But they don't stop racing. Not even for night meetings. Jockeys simply slip plastics over their silks and carry on through the downpour.

It was the second race on the card. I had drawn wide and as the gates sprung open my mount jumped sideways out of the barrier. The lateral movement unbalanced me and one foot almost came out of the iron. The field wasn't about to slow and wait for me to recover, so I regathered myself and started to push the horse along, driving forward while trying to wriggle my foot back into position. After 200 metres or so, we were travelling at a fair clip when I grabbed hold of the horse to find a handy position in the field. The sudden deceleration instantly forced my boot completely out of the iron. There was nothing to restrain my weight, least of all the slick surfaces of wet plastics and patent leather saddle. Like a wet cake of soap,

I shot off the horse. The landing spot wasn't the lush turf of Flemington or Randwick but Macau's sodden, sandy track which resembled a North Queensland mudflat just after the tide had gone out. Shoulder and head hit the ground together.

Crack!

A small explosion went off inside my head, followed by a burning sensation. I knew there and then that I had broken my neck. Fortunately, I was conscious and relatively clear-headed. With minimum movement, I eased off my helmet and lay straight on my back. The barrier attendants and starter, mainly Aussies, had sprinted from the gates as soon as they saw me fall.

'Don't move me,' I said through clenched teeth. 'I reckon I've broken my neck!'

The ambulance arrived, and I was carefully placed on a stretcher and loaded. Logic would dictate that, given the patient had a suspected neck injury, the ambulance would take me straight to hospital. But it was needed for the next race. So we rendezvoused with another ambulance, I was transferred and only then did we start the trip. Meanwhile, Sloane had been contacted and was on her way.

When you are living in another part of the world and an unscheduled event throws you off course, you have to prepare yourself for the unexpected. But nothing in my life could have readied me for the scene in accident and emergency. There are some things about Macau which are first rate, but the hospital system isn't one of them. Stretched out on a gurney, I was wheeled into a third-world version of the American TV show 'ER'. Coming from Australia, I was under the impression that a suspected broken neck would be given some sort of priority. It wasn't. Eventually, it looked like the staff were ready to give me some attention but the processing of patients was loudly interrupted by an infernal racket in the foyer. The remains of a violent gang battle had found its way to the hospital and was about to hijack what plans the accident and emergency staff had for that evening. Blood-splattered victims were lurching around, women were screaming and those well enough to summon the energy were shouting oaths of revenge and mayhem. It looked like a scene from a B-grade martial arts movie. But, this time, the blood wasn't fake. The screaming would die down and then start again as more victims arrived covered in blood. It was crazy. Meanwhile, I lay on a board, trying to keep perfectly still. The only parts that I dared move were my eyes to take in the uproar in the accident and emergency area. Chaos reigned. This wasn't a good situation. By this stage, I had been lying there for some time without anyone coming near me. Nobody had even bothered to wipe the mud and grime off me and the granules of sand wedged between my closely shaven head and the hard board were causing some pain and discomfort. The casualties from the gang battle had taken priority. The rest of us were shoved down the list.

Hours ticked by. Eventually, some sort of order was restored in accident and emergency, the blood mopped up and the screaming abated. Staff appeared by my side. Instructions were given. I was on my way to X-ray.

Soon I was in a room with a young doctor who was pegging the X-rays up on a light box.

'Hey, you've been lucky,' he said.

Lucky?

'You haven't broken it!' the doctor continued.

What? No way! This couldn't be right. I was certain something had snapped inside my neck. But here was a physician telling me that the X-rays indicated otherwise. At that point, I did get lucky. Fate intervened. An older doctor walked into the room and looked intently at the X-rays. He drew his young colleague to one side, spoke with him and then turned to me.

'We're sending you for a CAT scan,' he said.

It was well into the wee small hours of the morning and I was just about spent when the CAT scan results returned. By then I had been wheeled back to the emergency room and it was there that the older doctor appeared beside me with the news.

'Your neck is broken in two places,' he told me.

In any other instance, I might have shouted 'Told you so!'. But this was one time I would have preferred to be wrong.

At that point, the senior physician turned to his young charge and gave him one helluva blast. The lesson was well made because if I had taken the initial prognosis at face value, I might have stepped off the table, given my head a bit of a shake, snapped the spinal cord and ended up as a quadriplegic.

One simple turn of the head could have meant the difference between a stable fracture and a potentially fatal, unstable fracture. By keeping my head perfectly still the fracture had remained stable. The CAT scan showed that the second cervical vertebra, or the C2 – shaped like a butterfly or large moth – had been broken laterally, as well as fracturing across one of the 'wings'. But the brilliant news was that it had remained stable. With the right care it would heal.

SLOANE: 'I was at home in our flat and hadn't seen the race. The first I heard of the accident was when the wife of another Australian jockey, who was living in the same complex, phoned to say that Glen had been involved in a fall, and that he was okay but on his way to hospital. She would mind the kids while I went to join him. There had been talk among the Australians about how the hospital was not an ideal place to be. My intention was to get Glen out of there. I arrived to find him lying on a bed of sand that had stuck to him from the fall. A doctor told him that the X-rays showed there was no break and I think Glen might have been about to move when a nurse said, "Don't move until you know for sure." At first I was concerned but then relieved when I realised he could move his limbs and that meant he hadn't suffered any paralysis.'

From that point the news was both good and bad. Yes, I should make a full recovery but only after spending six month flat on my back in traction, unable to move. With no disrespect intended, one night in that hospital had been absolutely hellish. The prospect of spending the next six months of my life there pinned like an insect in an exhibition was too impossible to contemplate. I knew I wouldn't be able to last the distance. A bed was found. I was placed flat on my back while the nursing staff slipped on a neck brace. The long recovery process was about to start. Was this how I would spend the next six months of my life? No way. Sloane and I had already made up our minds that I wasn't staying.

Sometimes a refusal to accept what is assigned as your lot in life can be a godsend. There was a way out of the Macau hospital and Gary Moore would provide the key. The son of legendary Australian jockey George Moore was one of the region's top trainers and I had been riding for him during my time in Macau. His father-in-law, an eminent gynaecologist, was a close friend of a US- and Hong Kong-based specialist who happened to be an eminent orthopaedic surgeon with a distinguished international reputation. Dr Julian W Chang was the honorary medical advisor to the Sports Federation and Olympic Committee of Hong Kong, as well as Physician in Chief to the Hong Kong Olympic team. He was formerly Assistant Professor in orthopaedic surgery at the University of Rochester, New York, and Assistant Chief of orthopaedic service at Rochester General Hospital. I would later learn that he had treated footballers with similar injuries to mine.

Gary's wife Barbara put the wheels in motion, calls were made and a strategy put in place whereby I would get to see Dr Chang. There was only one hitch – he needed to see me in Hong Kong, not Macau. This would involve me leaving the hospital and catching a ferry from the mainland to Hong Kong. They might as well have asked me to fly to the moon. But, providing you were willing to pay the freight, there was a way. For an outlay of about three thousand Australian dollars, I engaged International SOS, the global medical evacuation team. These guys do not muck around. Within 24 hours they turned up at the Macau hospital, lifted me from the bed and placed me in what seemed like a large cocoon or sleeping bag. Then the cocoon was inflated until it filled every contour of my body, including the recesses in my ears, to the smallest millimetre, forming a protective shell which hugged me so tight that it was impossible to move. The best I could do was blink.

Like a mummy in a coffin, I was wheeled to a waiting ambulance and then driven down to the harbour to catch a ferry. I am not normally claustrophobic but this tomb presented a bit of a challenge. The weather was hot and humid, not the sort of day on which you would want to be trussed like a rolled roast. The sweat was pouring out of me and my carers were continually mopping my brow. Thankfully, Sloane was at my side offering her quiet reassurance and telling me to relax.

Now, travelling from Macau to Hong Kong involves a bit more than a simple ferry ride. We would have to pass through immigration. The team knew its business and had sent one of their number on ahead to have passports stamped and the paperwork completed. The ferry ride took an hour. Transport was waiting at the wharf and before long I was in a hospital bed in Hong Kong. Then, just as magically as they had appeared, the retrieval gang packed their equipment and left. Their job was done. As distracted as I was by my plight, I still couldn't help but be impressed by their efficiency and professionalism.

Two days had elapsed since the race fall and the situation had already taken a turn for the better. This time there was no waiting. Dr Chang was waiting to see me. He had copies of the CAT scans and ordered a new range of X-rays. While this was happening he was telling me about a rugby player he had treated. The injury was an almost identical break to mine but the difference was that the unfortunate footballer made the mistake of giving his head a shake just to check that his neck was okay. He would spend the rest of his life as a quadriplegic.

The good news was that I would not have to spend the next six months flat on my back waiting for the fractures to heal. Dr Chang told me there was a contraption called a halo brace, which would stabilise the head and neck to lock the site in place and allow the bones to knit. It sounded pretty barbaric and looked like a medieval instrument of torture. Four screws would be tapped into my skull to provide the stabilising foundation to support the brace. As for the brace itself, no self-respecting angel would be caught dead wearing this halo. When fitted, it looks like somebody has placed an inverted bar stool over your head. Walk down the street wearing this fashion accessory and you are bound to attract a few stares.

But there was no time to waste. I had arrived at the hospital at 4 pm and by 6 pm I was in theatre having local anaesthetic shots in my skull at the point where the first screw was to be inserted. The shots themselves were an ordeal as the needle has to penetrate bone. Once the site was ready, the surgeon slid the titanium brace underneath me and started screwing the first of four points into place.

Penetrating the skin was okay but once the screw hit harder matter things began to get interesting. I don't know what the most awful sound in the world might be but the racket steel makes when it is screwing through bone is right up there. Think of nails on a blackboard but a whole lot closer to home.

The screw had to be exactly the right tension. This was achieved by a ratcheting process. Every time the surgeon cranked the ratchet another notch a lightning bolt of pure pain shot right through me. One down, three to go!

The exercise took about an hour and by the time the third screw was going in I was just about accepting the pain. If Frankenstein's monster could put up with it, so could I. Once the screws were stationed, the four rods – like the legs of a bar stool – were put into place.

The critical point of this process was getting the head locked in exactly the right position so that the fractured areas line up perfectly. A bit like trying to glue together pieces of broken china. This was achieved courtesy of another session of CAT scans. With my help and constant references to the scans, Dr Chang positioned my head in exactly the right place so that the lines of the fracture would correspond.

Two-and-half hours after starting the procedure, he had me up walking with the assistance of a walking frame. It was a miracle! The contraption towered above me, staked as it was to the four screws in my skull and preventing even the most minimal movement of the head. In fact, my head was as rigid as a pylon of the Sydney Harbour Bridge and would remain that way until the bones knitted.

With no way of being able to move my noggin, it soon became obvious how much we rely on head and neck movement as an important part of the balancing process, particularly when we're walking. I would have to get used to walking without moving my head. That evening, I kept doing laps of the corridor until I discarded the walking frame. Finally, the nursing staff eased me into bed where I was introduced to the routine that would be my sleeping position for the next four months: propped upright supported by pillows.

In Macau, the prognosis had been six months in hospital flat on my back. In Hong Kong, I was discharged after just two days – long enough to see that everything had settled, the halo was properly in place and for Sloane to learn how to clean the screw holes in my head.

A nurse accompanied us on the ferry ride back to Macau. I wasn't exactly the Elephant Man but the halo brace high over my head sure gave our fellow passengers something to look at. We would need a week in Macau to tidy up our affairs before heading home to Australia. For the invalid, it was a week of deep reflection. Never in my life had I felt so alert and clear-headed. There was time to think about what might have been. Dr Chang had told us that I had been a millimetre or so from severing my spinal chord. What survival instinct had told me to keep still? If I had turned my head as little as 10 degrees I would have ended up in the morgue, rather than the hospital.

It dawned on me that I had been given a second chance. Back in Macau, when Sloane finally brought the kids into see me, the tears started flowing. I knew there and then that this second chance was not to be wasted. I would be the best father I could possibly be. And I would do my utmost to be a better person. For too long I had been at war with the world, the ultra-competitive kid who was never satisfied, who went through life perpetually convinced his glass was half empty, never half full. Well, from that moment on, that guy was gone. I felt a sense of calm, an unimaginable burst of warm energy. Sometimes, when we do not heed a thousand warnings or hints, the fates have to throw us a really big one to make us sit up and finally take notice. That's what I felt had happened to me. This time, I would heed the tap on the shoulder.

10

The Tin Man learns
a lesson

While awaiting the flight home, I convalesced at the home of Australian trainer and former jockey Peter Leyshon and his wife Michelle. They were just the tonic we needed. In that wonderful Aussie way of making light of almost any circumstances, Peter treated the whole episode as a bit of a joke. Just when I might have succumbed to the crushing concern of wondering whether I would make it back to full health, let alone ride again, he had a beautiful knack of keeping everything light-hearted. His catchcry for the day was 'Pub opens at 12!' and on the stroke of noon he would appear with a round of drinks. I can't imagine a better host for keeping everything upbeat and optimistic.

Privately, I was already starting to set my own goals. As soon as I suffered the injury, my thoughts went to Sloane and the kids. Would I be all right? Would they be all right? Then, my very next thought was: 'Is this going to cost me the ride on The Lass?'

Waiting for me back in Australia was the horse with the brilliance to be the boom galloper for the approaching spring and beyond. Republic Lass was her name and she figured enormously in my plans. A beautiful filly by Canny Lad out of Swift Seasons, she was trained by Guy Walter who suspected that he just might have a champion on his hands. I was given a glimpse of her enormous potential shortly before heading off to Macau when The Lass collected her first Group 1 victory with a scorching win in the Australian Jockey Club Oaks at Randwick. At that point, she still had plenty of growing to do and both Guy and I shared the view that she would develop into a great racing mare. Broken neck, or no broken neck, I was determined that I would not relinquish the ride. My motives were not merely selfish. The prospect of sharing Group 1 success with an honest, hardworking trainer like Guy Walter made the deal especially appealing.

When I first landed in Sydney, it had taken me a while to get to know Guy. We might have had more to do with each other in my early time in Sydney if it weren't for the fact that I was based at Kensington and his stable was at Warwick Farm. As a horseman he deserved the deepest respect. You would never hear Guy wishing for something in a horse that wasn't there. Instead, he always played with the cards he was dealt. No matter the quality of the horse, Guy could look at it and determine its true capability. It gave him a reputation for welcoming an unheralded animal into his stable, putting the hard work in and then turning it out as a winner. His ability to transform a horse in short time from an unheralded performer to a Group 1 winner was uncanny. After a while, he did it with such frequency that we ceased to be shocked. He was especially gifted when it came to getting the best out of fillies and mares.

Guy's planning was meticulous, particularly in the way he took a horse through the grades to achieve the ultimate goal. Few trainers invested as much thought into the business of identifying every scrap of ability in a galloper. Inevitably, he would come up with the goods. From a jockey's perspective, I found him wonderful to work with because he would involve you in the project of moulding a piece of putty into a Group winner. He was my kind of trainer and Republic Lass was my kind of horse. It occurred to me that if Guy Walter had the opportunity to train on his own private facility with its own track, he would become one of the best. He and his wife Wendy worked very closely together and he has a tremendous rapport with his staff. He never bagged a jockey for a ride but always placed total trust in what the rider had to offer. In so many ways, just by how he went about his business, he taught me a lot. Therefore I had great incentive to get back in the saddle for Guy as quickly as possible.

The original prognosis indicated my neck would take a minimum six months to heal. The other possibilities were that it could need even longer – say eight to 12 months – or that it would never recover properly to allow me to resume race riding. The only thought that I dared entertain was the most positive outcome. Forget about never riding again – in order to be ready for the approaching spring, I knew I had to be recovered inside four months. I looked at the six-month timeframe mapped out by my carers and simply cut it in half. My goal was to be back in three months. Constructing a mental picture of that period in my head, I zeroed in on a particular date and skewered it as my deadline.

The first giant step on the road to recovery meant getting us all back to Australia and familiar surrounds where Sloane and the kids could return to near-normality and I could avail myself of a carefully planned rehabilitation program.

What Sloane did to get us back to Australia was little short of a miracle. The broken jockey in the spaceman's outfit was next to useless. Luckily, a team of friends swarmed around, helped us scoop up our mountain of luggage plus two tiny kids and transported the lot to Hong Kong airport for the flight back to Sydney. With an excess baggage bill totalling $2000, we looked like we were moving house.

SLOANE: 'That trip home was one of the most difficult things I've ever done in my life. We had two tiny kids and Glen in that contraption. It was scary, a very barbaric-looking apparatus. People stopped and stared, some made jokes and others just laughed. It was awful.'

Making it through the metal detectors with a meccano set on top of my head might have been a bit of a joke but for the fact that I wasn't exactly in the best physical shape or frame of mind for a long-haul flight. As I shuffled aboard, trying to ignore the stares of fellow passengers, a young man in the queue caught my eye.

'I had one of those contraptions on my head,' he said.

'Really?'

'Yep. A snow-skiing accident. What about the pain you go through when they're fitting it?'

I smiled ruefully at the memory.

'Don't worry,' he said. 'It's no big deal. I'm fine now.'

Buoyed by his words and the feeling that I was by no means alone on this strange journey, I found my seat and settled in for the ride. As the aircraft lifted off the tarmac, so did my hopes that everything would eventually work out all right.

Back in Sydney I came under the professional care of orthopaedic surgeon Dr Ian Farey at Royal North Shore Hospital. He had a reputation for working with athletes, particularly footballers with spinal injuries, impatient to resume their careers as soon as possible. When I laid out my timeframe and made it clear that there could be no compromise he looked at me for a moment and then got straight down to business. We were on the same track right from the outset.

Dr Farey scheduled me for a series of visits to monitor my progress and then sent me home. After the ordeal of suffering the injury, hospitalisation, the fitting of the brace and the perils of travel, the temptation might have been to head home and simply slump for a month or two. But I had other plans. Firstly, I had to preserve my fitness. So I started on a daily regimen of walking around my neighbourhood, slowly at first and then at a more brisker pace until I was certain that the anaerobic effect was starting to tell. Having been away for so long, there were plenty of chores to do around home, including a bit of landscaping. I built a rock wall by hand, lifting and barrowing the stones and then levering them into place with a crowbar. All the while, the halo brace stayed perfectly in place, locking my neck and head in a fixed position and giving me the sort of body language reminiscent of the Tin Man from 'The Wizard of Oz'.

When something as dramatic as a career-ending injury befalls you, one thing is sure and certain: you find out just which friends are of the fair-weather kind and who will remain true blue.

Information is the currency of the racing game. The gambling world would give an arm and a leg to get inside the heads of jockeys, trainers and anyone close to the performance end of the game. For that reason most of us have to be pretty vigilant about who we let inside our circle of friendship and trust. Don't get me wrong, racing is an extremely social world and there are acquaintances galore. But when it comes down to knowing exactly who you can trust, most of us are very selective.

Bob Stanton, former professional golfer and true friend, would prove one of my greatest supporters on the road back from the neck injury. When he was young, Bob won the Australian PGA and had some success in the United States. Today he will be the first to tell you that he succumbed to the party life and never realised his potential as a player. Those who know him best say that he was an unbelievable talent. Now in his 60s, he can still swing it with the best and on any good day can still break par.

As a friend and a decent human being, Bob would claim a spot in the hall of fame.

We met not long after I arrived in Sydney and struck up a friendship which grew into a genuine bond. Bob had travelled extensively and experienced the sort of highs and lows of life and business that tend to add up to hard-won wisdom.

At the time I was still a young bloke a long way from home. Subconsciously, I might have been looking for a father-figure to help provide some guidance. He became the person I could confide in and ask questions of. And, without any mucking about, he always had the answer. In time, Bob became someone worthy of my total trust.

Golf is a great excuse for a stroll and a chat. As an insight into someone's personality the game can be very revealing. The Glen Boss that revealed himself to Bob Stanton on the golf course was a pretty headstrong young man with a short fuse, especially when things didn't go exactly to plan. Over time, the worldly-wise, older bloke would help me deal with that side of my personality. Out on the course we would talk about a whole range of issues and I would go away having learned something valuable.

Bob has been there through my major victories and my lowest times. He was there for the recuperation from the broken neck. In fact, during that period when I was at a low point, we flew up to Port Douglas to stay with Bob and his wife Lucy. His wise counsel was invaluable in helping me focus on my recovery. He has always given me great advice and a few kicks up the arse when I've needed them and the recovery process was no exception. When the opportunity to play golf in Port Douglas bobbed up, I accepted Bob's invitation, boarded the aircraft for Queensland and ploughed around the Mirage course. The experts will tell you that one of the secrets to striking a golf ball sweetly is to keep your head perfectly still. The old halo brace certainly had that aspect well and truly nailed. Luckily, with all that metal hanging over my head, there were no electrical storms in the vicinity.

By keeping busy I not only retained some level of fitness but helped the time fly. Yet, I was still impatient about the rate of progress.

'I'll give you another four weeks in this thing,' said Dr Farey. I was back in his rooms for a regular check-up when he brought the timeframe right back into focus.

'How about two?' I suggested.

The specialist must have thought that I had rushed things enough. Instead of settling on my deadline, we agreed that I would return a week later and he would give me a date. At the next appointment he suggested it would need three more weeks. I wasn't having it.

'No way,' I said. 'How about one more week?'

Seven days later I returned. Dr Farey had either succumbed to my impatience or was convinced that the halo brace had served its purpose. It was time to unwind the screws.

After months in that contraption I could understand how the man in the iron mask must have felt when he poked his beak out into fresh air for the first time. Once the apparatus was removed, Dr Farey sent me for X-rays which revealed a perfect re-alignment and knit of the fractured bones. He was amazed at the perfection of Dr Chang's handiwork. It would have been difficult to imagine a better result.

'How do you feel,' he asked.

'Pretty good,' I replied.

'Do you want to move?'

Now, this was the tricky bit. What if there were some tiny spurs on the line of the fracture? On top of that, my neck didn't really want to move. Inactivity had tightened ligaments, tendons and wasted muscles. I made a rather pathetic effort at moving my head through a few degrees.

'No, if you're going to be like that,' said Dr Farey, 'I'll knock you out and move it myself. Believe me, you're not going to hurt it.'

Slowly, I rotated my head. He stood behind me cupping my cranium, gently manipulating my head on its axis.

'It's up to you,' he said, 'how far you want to take it.'

My confidence soared.

'I need to be back riding track work in two to three weeks,' I told him.

'That's rushing it but, as I said, it's up to you,' responded Dr Farey.

The next phase of my rehabilitation involved intense physio-therapy on my neck and shoulders. Under the coaxing of expert massaging they began to respond, weakly at first but with more strength and flexibility as the sessions continued.

With the halo brace gone I jumped on the scales and weighed myself. Believe it or not, I had retained my riding weight of 53 kilograms. Throughout the convalescence I had eaten well and exercised regularly. The combination of healthy food, healthy activity and quality rest had speeded up my recovery. But I am convinced that it was my positive mind-set, targeting a goal and doing everything in my power to achieve the objective, that had made the difference.

Straightaway, I started making calls, ringing Guy Walter and other trainers and owners telling them that I would soon be back. Nobody could have blamed them if they had given up on Glen Boss. They had seen the news reports, heard the shocking details of how I had broken my neck and how the doctors didn't expect me back inside six months, if at all. Plus, they had seen the photos of me in the halo brace on my return to Sydney. Riding racehorses is a risky enough business without resorting to the services of a busted-up jockey. But, to their eternal credit, most of them stuck by me, accepting my assurances that I would be back as good, no, better, than ever.

The day finally dawned when I would be back on a racehorse for the first time since that fateful night in Macau. I made the drive from our family home in north-west Sydney, where we'd moved to about a year earlier, through the dark streets to

Randwick. It was a journey of sweet redemption, a ride back to the familiar embrace of my first love. I was infused with a warm inner glow and a sense of joyous relief that I had truly been given a second chance.

On that first morning I rode slow work, just cantering and trotting around with the irons set a bit longer than usual. The next day, I turned up at Randwick, jumped up on a horse and in no time had it into a gallop. Track work was back on my agenda and I was wasting no time. But my legs were sore that week. Muscle wastage had taken its toll during my time off. There are muscles you bring into play when riding a horse and they have to be kept in tune. My return to race riding was not far away but there was one hurdle that had to be overcome before I would don the silks again. It was imperative that I be able to handle the power translated when a horse surges from the barrier. For that reason, I made a point of riding in barrier trials before confirming my return to a full race meeting.

Three weeks after the halo brace was removed, the name of Glen Boss re-appeared among the list of engaged jockeys. There was no intention of easing my way back into the business – I intended to hit the ground running and did just that by riding a winner at my first meeting. I was calm, focused, totally switched on to the job and without a single trace of doubt. Was I afraid? I was sore and tired after the day's racing. But never afraid. Not for a moment.

I was back.

11

The turning point

With time, friends and associates began to notice what I already suspected. The Glen Boss who had stepped out of the halo brace was a different Glen Boss to the one who had travelled to Macau those months before. That bloke used to be uptight, moody, impatient and often aggressive. The new fella was calmer, more relaxed with himself and those around him.

For years I had been hard on others who fell short of my expectations. But, most of all, I had been hard on myself. In the time since the fall my priorities had changed. I still loved racing as much, if not more, than ever, but I could have let it go. In making the decision to not hang on to my passion like grim death, it became a much easier and more amenable companion and assumed a different place in my existence. Before, my priority had been a hard-nosed drive to be the best. Now, my family stood clear and bright at the top of my list of priorities.

In Macau, all the things that weren't important had been

stripped away. Since then, racing became more of a game, something to be loved and enjoyed. Why had I started riding in the first place? Because it was fun. It wasn't about money or glory; it was simply fun. So I set about getting back to the pure and clear reason why I rode gallopers. In so doing, I stopped taking myself so seriously. Now I think that reflects in the way I ride.

Before the Macau fall, I would get tense simply by doing the homework on my race rides and that tension would build. In reality, I was just collecting baggage. It made me too intense; it convinced me that being a jockey was my whole life.

The time of clear thought that ensued after the fall allowed me to strip my existence down to its simple truths. In so doing I found real clarity and the ability to relax. The amazing by-product of this clearer vision and lighter attitude is that it made me a better jockey. It has allowed me to operate more on instinct. The more relaxed you are the quicker your brain can process complex issues. In this way it has given me an insight as to how truly great athletes operate. If you watch a Tiger Woods or a Michael Jordan it appears that they are performing at half speed but, in fact, they are operating faster and more efficiently than the rest. The relaxed mind operates on instinct allowing everything you have learned through training and practice to flow naturally through your game.

The only way to reach that point is by relaxing and trusting in the foundation of work and training. In this mode, the brain unconsciously takes over. For me, it seems like the brain is actually working way out in front of events, pre-empting what is about to take place and preparing me for what happens next. Once I made that conscious decision to relax it became so simple. Automatic. Before, I'd be thinking: 'Are they going too fast, too slow, should I be somewhere else, am I in the right position?' And, before you can digest all that, it's too late. Now I don't even think about the race. I've done my homework the night before and now I just let it happen. People talk about plan A and B, etc. I don't plan. Instead, I get a little mental picture in my head and, from that point, ad lib. In racing, when you have a plan, perhaps one in 20 times it works out that way. Those odds tell me that I am better off taking it as it comes.

Being relaxed has made me more intuitive. I can spot trouble before it happens and take measures to avoid it. I know exactly how fast or slow the horse I'm riding should be going. I know exactly where I should be at certain points in a race, and without even thinking about it, my mount is positioned where it needs to be.

Pace – the art of knowing at what speed you are riding – is one of the most crucial factors of all. If the speed is on in a race, you know they have gone too quick and will come back to you. If they are going too slow, you know you have to step it up, providing you are in a position to do something about it. As a kid, I started with a stopwatch – one thousand, two thousand . . . counting it out. In Hong Kong bar codes on individual horses tripped the timing devices, so there was no room for guesswork. That experience sharpened my ability even more. Now it comes automatically. I have always prided myself on being a pretty good judge of pace. Some jockeys call it 'the clock in the head'. Since the fall and my new approach to riding, it is no longer a clock. Instead, it is just a feeling – an intuition. Some horses have different strides and might feel like they are going quicker, but my sixth sense never fails me. If there is a slight change of pace, I can pick it straightaway. I know for a fact that there are some jockeys who can't – they have no idea. The answer to the pace puzzle comes naturally to some; others have to work at it and others never get it. Too many young jockeys work on their style in the belief that it is the most fundamental part of their riding. While they are worrying about how good they look on the horse, they are often ignoring the value of understanding pace.

As I've said before, riding a racehorse is like driving a Formula One car. The pace puzzle is how to get that car first across the line on the very last drop of petrol. In other words, maximising its total energy potential during the course of the race. Every horse is different. Every race is different. The complexity of the riddle can keep you awake at night and drive you crazy . . . unless you can find a way to relax and allow your training and intuition to just let it happen.

For a long time now trainers have come to trust what I do. Sometimes they might say, 'Jump and lead because there's going to be no speed' but I already know all that. Most of the top trainers ask me what I want to do. I say relax, you've done everything to get the horse right, now it's my time. Worry does you no good, especially worrying about things over which you've got no control. Sit back in the stand, relax and enjoy.

12

The wins start coming

It started to snowball.

Good form leads to more offers to ride quality horses. Good form plus quality horses produces winners. Perhaps it was my new attitude or growing maturity, or maybe it was a combination of both, but owners and trainers began to ask my advice more than in the past. Now when you see a trainer talking to me before the race, chances are we're discussing dinner reservations rather than race tactics. I much prefer trainers who don't give me race instructions but let me work it out for myself. If I erred during a race ride, I would come back and tell the connections that I had stuffed up. The more I placed my trust in my own homework and race instincts, the easier it all became.

The most Group 1 winners I had racked up in a season was four during 1995–96. In 1998–99 I came close to eclipsing that personal best but could not manage a fifth victory. However, there were better days ahead.

The prospect of ever riding another Group 1 winner must have looked a real long shot when I was in a squalid Macau hospital with a broken neck. Four months later, I was aboard Shot Of Thunder in the Toorak Handicap (1600 metres) at Caulfield, daring to think what a great day this would be if I could notch my first big race win since my comeback and, at the same time, deliver the first Group 1 victory for John O'Shea, a fellow Queenslander and one of the trainers who had retained his faith in me.

John O'Shea was very much in the Guy Walter's mould, only younger. He rated as the best of the new generation of trainers. He had certainly paid his dues having worked for Bart and served as a foreperson for Gai. That experience imbued him with the knowledge of horseflesh and the work ethic required at the top level.

Like Guy he was an absolute perfectionist, leaving nothing to chance in the pursuit of realising every bit of potential in a horse. Timing is a mark of all great trainers and when John O'Shea stepped a horse up to the Group 1 mark and told you it was ready, you could believe it was spot on. As with most passionate people, he was very intense and expected everyone around him to bring the same commitment to the job. When you worked with John you had to keep stepping up to the mark. That suited me perfectly because it left no room for complacency and was conducive to bringing out the best in me.

We enjoyed a great relationship because we shared the same ideals and were headed in the same direction. Despite his intensity, I would find John an immensely kind person who never dwelt on the quality of a ride. If my performance had been below par, he would make a comment and move straight on. In that way, he was an absolute straightshooter. You knew where you stood. There were no 'maybe's' with John. He would never rattle on about 'we might put you on that horse'. Instead, he would tell you straight up whether you're riding it or not. If he took you off a horse, he would give you the exact reason – no bull. There are many people in the business who could take a leaf out of John's book – call it like it is and get on with the game.

The prospect of coming back from the broken neck and partnering John O'Shea for his maiden Group 1 was great motivation. Shot Of Thunder, the subject of a betting plunge that brought it in from $7 to $4.80, was considered more than a good chance, provided the jockey could get the job done.

In a thrilling finish, I managed to find a gap down the centre of the track to edge out Scenic Peak by a nose. The veteran Umrum was half a neck away with Pernod a short half-head back in fourth place. After a double protest, Scenic Peak was relegated to fourth with Umrum elevated to second and Pernod getting third. Messrs Boss and O'Shea weren't bothered with protests – we were too busy celebrating the breaking of our own personal droughts.

Although the spring of 2002 produced no more big wins, it was still great to be back in racing fettle and realise, ride by ride, that there were no lingering effects from the neck fractures. My optimism grew with the prospect of being reunited with Republic Lass in the autumn.

In late March the Sydney turf scene was abuzz with the first appearance in the harbour city of the dual Cox Plate winner, the mighty West Australian, Northerly. While there was little doubt who would start favourite in the Group 1 Ranvet Stakes at Rosehill, there was a ripple of speculation about the champion's ability to handle the reverse way of going at his first start in the clockwise direction. There had been talk that Northerly might be susceptible as he had shown a tendency in Melbourne to lay in, or veer towards the inside rail, when put under pressure. But trainer Fred Kersley was making no excuses: 'A champion can run in a saucer,' he said. A win by Northerly would lift his tally of Group 1 victories to 10 – just three behind the champion mare Sunline and four behind the record holder Kingston Town.

I had chased Northerly's tail on a few occasions and had yet to identify a weakness. He was too good a horse and I knew he would adapt. If anyone was going to topple him they would have to do it on sheer merit, not luck. My strategy on Republic Lass was to forget about Northerly. Instead, I would concentrate on giving The Lass the best possible chance of being able to run home strongly over the final furlong. If that wasn't good enough to beat him, then so be it.

When the horses had started and settled down in the Ranvet, Manner Hill went to an early lead with jockey Paddy Payne slotting Northerly into second, a length away and one off the fence. At the six-furlong mark, I noticed the pace quicken as Freemason made a surge from the back to take up the running. It left Republic Lass back in last place, but I reminded myself patience was the key.

Those who had backed the West Aussie horse roared their approval when the big gelding swept to the lead halfway down the straight. The sight of the champion showing Sydney his form meant few spotted the story emerging back in the pack. Republic Lass was on her way. Like a whirlwind gathering up everything in its path, she reeled them in until, at the 300-metre mark, she was abreast of Northerly. This is the pure essence of racing: a four-year-old filly at her peak having the temerity to race up alongside a six-year-old gelding and proven champion and eyeball him in a dogfight to the line. My strategy had been to preserve every drop of energy The Lass had in her tank for this last mighty challenge. Now we would find out just which thoroughbred would claim the day as the two great gallopers went head-to-head for the line. One reason outstanding horses win races is that they simply hate to be passed. Rising to the challenge, Northerly fought back like a true champion. But Republic Lass dug deep. She simply refused to be intimidated and forged on to score a truly memorable victory by the skinny margin of a short half-head. It was great to be back and I made it absolutely clear to Guy Walter how much it had meant to have him entrust his brilliant filly to the bloke with the busted neck. My impression of Republic Lass had been confirmed: she was capable of greatness and I had to pinch myself at the realisation that I had first call on her services.

The Ranvet was only my third Group 1 win since returning but, in so many ways, it meant the world to me.

Choisir is French for 'to choose' and what a choice the brilliant chestnut colt by Danehill Dancer out of Great Selection turned out to be for the international reputation of Australian racing and Broadmeadow-based trainer Paul Perry. He was all power, a broad bundle of bone and muscle with a withering turn of speed that would take him to the very heights of the game.

In June 2003 Paul saddled him up on the Tuesday and again on the Saturday at England's Royal Ascot carnival. Choisir ran a class field off its feet in the Group 2 King's Stand Stakes to make a mockery of his 25–1 starting price and then backed this up by breaking the track record in the Group 1 Golden Jubilee Stakes. At season's end he was named Australia's Champion International Performer.

My moment of glory on the history-making colt had occurred in the previous February. The big chestnut was chasing his fifth win when a very smart field lined up for the Group 1 Lightning Stakes, a classic sprint down the Flemington straight. The honour of riding the future international champion had fallen to yours truly. Choisir, who had a reputation as a strong-minded colt, was having his first run back from a spell. Conventional logic says the grandstand side of the track is the quickest. Instead, I took him to the inside where he relished the opportunity to race alone, powering to an unbeatable lead and winning by three-quarters of a length from Spinning Hill who, in turn, was three lengths clear of the rest of the field.

My perils in Macau had been well documented in Brisbane where I had done so much of my earlier race riding. So, while Choisir settled into his English surrounds, I was hopeful that the return to familiar territory would do the trick when I touched down in Brisbane for the Queensland winter carnival.

Private Steer was having only her 10th race start and she had made it into the field for the rich Group 1 Stradbroke Handicap with the light weight of just 48 kilograms. Retaining the ride on the brilliant filly meant a considerable sacrifice on my part – shedding almost five kilograms in a desperate effort to make the weight.

Fasting and sweating it out in the sauna can do things to your head and it made me recall Malcolm Johnston's favourite wasting story. A natural lightweight, Mal rarely resorted to the sauna but would delight in appearing at the window munching on a cream bun while another jockey sweated it out inside.

Private Steer made a nonsense of the light weight by outclassing the capacity field. It was great to be back in Brisbane.

Maguire, with Chris Munce aboard, started favourite for the

Brisbane Cup but snapped a leg in running and was later put down. On the David Hall–trained Piachay and much farther back than intended, I was lucky to evade Maguire as the stricken galloper fell back through the field. We were handy enough if the breaks came our way and, when an opening appeared in the straight, I knew my 12–1 chance would finish it off. Two Group 1 victories was a wonderful way to celebrate my return to the Sunshine State.

That first season back delivered five Group 1 victories – equal to my best. But, more importantly, it convinced me that the rebuilt Glen Boss was a different jockey. Since returning, I was more relaxed. Almost as if by magic, I had freed myself from the anxiety generated by my own unrealistic expectations. It enabled me to think more clearly and focus so much better on the task. It meant my preparation for big races and carnivals in particular was more methodical, less stressful and more productive. Miraculously, a formula for how to be at my best in big races had identified itself.

In earlier years I had been very much my own man, believing that there was little I could learn from the world beyond racing. But, after Macau, all that changed. My antennae had been re-tuned. One individual who would help me greatly with that process by broadening my horizons and showing that there are always exciting new challenges to be met was John Brown. The former butcher and one-time Federal Minister for Tourism and Sport and chairman of Australia's Tourism Taskforce was well past retirement age when we first met but had more energy than blokes a quarter of his age. He had packed so much living and achievement into one life that his CV must have be as long as Randwick straight. Others knew him for his tireless work on behalf of numerous charities.

Bobby Stanton introduced us and it was immediately apparent John knew way more than the average turf lover. I had not been long in Sydney and it was great to make an acquaintance who was incredibly well connected, had a genuine love for the sport and enjoyed a bet. In subsequent years I would learn to value his judgement and wisdom on a whole range of subjects.

Brownie was always thinking about somebody else which explained in part why he spent so much of his time on charitable endeavours. He always told me how fortunate he was when compared to so many other people. Helping others was the great hobby of his life. Those who knew him had so much respect for him. Again, he was one of those characters great to be around. John possessed the traits I admire: a 110 per cent man, who would never run from a fight and was intensely loyal to his friends.

He was a mine of wordly wisdom and I would regularly turn to him for career guidance and business advice. Like Bob, he never minced words. Having survived the world of politics, if a tough message needed to be imparted, Brownie would go straight to the heart of the matter. He would have made a formidable opponent – very strong and forthright. Among the people I held respect for he was up there with the best. If any of us could make it to the grave having lived a life half as large and productive as John Brown's, you'd be pretty content.

The business of being matched with quality horses is not a game of chance. I spend countless hours doing my homework, studying the breeding, watching the results of the yearling sales, scrutinising how young horses fare in their barrier trials and talking constantly to trainers and owners. In recent years all this work has really paid off. At one stage, I did my sums and figured that, of the top 15 horses in Australia, I was riding eight of them.

Agents also have a vital role to play in securing the best rides for the jockeys they represent. Sometimes an agent will approach a jockey with a proposal to represent him. Sometimes it's the jockey who approaches the agent. Early in my career I was represented by the Gold Coast–based agent Michael O'Brien who did a fantastic job before he moved to Hong Kong to further his career. Then I had a few ups and downs before Alan 'Hats' Aitken took the role on. Hats had a brilliant mind for remembering form and did an outstanding job on my behalf before he too was lured to Hong Kong. Greg Harris, brother of former jockey Wayne Harris, represented me for three years. Then he was followed by the best in the business, Bryan Haskins.

All the homework by me and lobbying by my agents would eventually pay off by placing me on a collection of outstanding horses. The results show that during season 2003–04 we had made some smart choices, although it didn't look that way when word came through that Private Steer had succumbed to injury. As we headed into October, Metropolitan Day at Randwick presented a chance to put a smile back on the face of John O'Shea, who was doubtlessly hurting over the loss of Private Steer. Yet my hopes of riding a winner for him in the Metrop didn't look too promising when I was writhing in agony on the turf after having my knee jammed against the barriers early in the day. However, five races later, the knee was the last thing on my mind as John and I agreed on the race tactics for his Metrop chance Bedouin. The stayer had been unlucky in his previous races so we both figured that riding him quietly and hoping for the runs to come in the straight might offer the best strategy. To our collective joy, the race panned out exactly as planned. In his usual magnanimous way, John was unstinting in his praise of my ride. It was his third Group 1 winner and I took quiet pride in having landed all three.

The Melbourne spring carnival had never been fertile ground for my ambitions so I was more than thrilled to kick off Cup week by winning the LKS Mackinnon Stakes on Casual Pass. This time, the tactics were almost the opposite of what was required to win the Metrop on Bedouin. Lee Freedman's Caulfield Cup winner Mummify was the early leader, but the slow pace was never going to do Casual Pass any favours. I hadn't gone into the race with a firm plan, preferring to see what developed and take my chances accordingly. Needs dictated that we get to the lead and play catch-us-if-you-can. I knew Casual Pass had plenty of speed and that if he could get out front and relax, he would be very hard to catch. The gelding strode to the lead and did it very easily for the next 800 metres. Into the straight and we were still three lengths clear. The question was: had I judged the pace well enough or would we be swamped in the shadows of the post? I knew the older stayers in the race would be finishing fast on the outside, among them Pentastic who was arriving like a cloudburst. If he grabbed us before the line the critics could rightly say that I went too early. In this case the margin between good and bad judgement on my part was a half-head as Casual Pass became the first three-year-old in 55 years to win the race.

Garry Newham and I went back a long way. Like me, he was from the rough end of the racing game, a former quarter-horse trainer who had turned up on the Gold Coast about 15 years before with a stable boasting one thoroughbred. About the same time, a kid from Caboolture was also chancing his arm on the Coast. Garry and I enjoyed a bit of luck together and his stable grew. Perusing my 2004 chances for Group 1 success in the Chipping Norton Stakes at Warwick Farm, it was pretty gratifying to find myself on the best horse Garry had ever had in his care, the brilliant Starcraft. It wasn't the strongest weight-for-age field in Australia, but Starcraft was simply too good.

Heading into the Sydney Easter carnival, my tally of Group 1 wins had risen to 30. It was a worthy record but still pretty humble alongside the 119 the incomparable George Moore managed to stuff into his saddlebags from a stellar career, or the 108 racked up by the great Roy Higgins. On the list of great Australian riders, Glen Boss was still a long way down the rankings.

My view is that you can only play what is in front of you and I was convinced the Easter carnival was absolutely ripe with opportunity. I had some outstanding rides and my frame of mind, fitness and focus were better than ever. I had always prided myself on my physical condition but somewhere during the transformation of the previous year, the challenge of getting myself absolutely primed for the major carnivals had taken on a new dimension. Distractions seemed to melt away allowing mind and body to work together. In some ways, I would compare it to the process a professional boxer goes through in preparing himself for a title fight. Consequently, when the autumn carnival of '04 rolled around, I felt primed to take on the world.

It nearly didn't happen. A two-meeting suspension for care-less riding meant that I would miss the first day of the carnival on Saturday 10 April. Later, the suspension was halved on appeal, clearing me to ride at Randwick. Chris Munce was not so lucky. A suspension cost him the ride on Gai Waterhouse's Golden Slipper winner Dance Hero, favourite for the Group 1 AJC Sires' Produce Stakes. Every top jockey has stories about losing winning rides through suspension, or picking them up from other jockeys' misfortune. As with Flying Spur in the Slipper years before, Dance Hero presented me with a Group 1 victory on another outstanding two year old.

My desperation to have the suspension reduced had much to do with my wish to stick with Starcraft in the feature race of the day, the AJC Australian Derby. I knew he was a magnificent specimen and the weight-for-age classic over 2400 metres was just the race to show his true worth. By the end of Derby day the 54,000 fans packed into Randwick would be of the same view.

The day had the potential to be a victorious homecoming for owner Paul Makin who had grown up in the Randwick area and had picked up Starcraft for $80,000 as a yearling in New Zealand. But first we had to win the race from a field which included VRC Oaks' winner Special Harmony and Lonhro's little brother, Niello, who was going for the treble, having won the Rosehill and Canterbury Guineas in brilliant fashion.

On settling down, Starcraft relaxed when I parked him on the fence with a little more than half of the field in front of us. The only problem was that the long shot Braeloch, rated to near perfection by Danny Beasley, had cleared out with the full intention of pinching the Derby from the favoured runners. We eased off the fence towards the middle of the track and

Starcraft responded like a champion. From the barrier to the post he raced beautifully. He did everything I asked of him and that was enough as we nabbed Braeloch in the last few strides to win by a long head.

13

What a week!

Monday 12 April 2004. Private Steer had a huge stature as a racehorse and she went into the Doncaster at Randwick as the raging favourite. A rumour that she was carrying an injury caused the bookmakers to take her on and the money came flooding in. I had assured John O'Shea that we would be outside the first six and inside the first 10 starters on settling down. But no sooner had we jumped than Private Steer got smashed and shunted back to second last. We started driving forward again looking for a mid-field spot but, by the time the field had travelled 600 metres, we had had copped no less than three bad checks. At the 800-metre mark we were a conspicuous last. My first thought was: 'What is John going to be thinking about all this!' Anyone who backed Private Steer would have had their head in their hands. Then, a feeling of calm came over me and I thought: 'Whoa, relax, chill.' At that point I went into auto pilot. 'Trust her ability and trust yourself,' I told myself. That feeling of calm is a great feeling to have. Everything goes very quiet. My understanding is that it's what some athletes call 'The Zone'. You hear but don't hear, see but don't see. It's like being in another place.

My mind was as clear and calm as a sheet of ice. Patience. With the entire field still in front of Private Steer, I began to count: 'One, two, three . . .' On 10 I let her go.

At the top of the rise on Randwick's famous straight, the 2004 Doncaster field had taken on a familiar sight. Gai Waterhouse, who had saddled up six Doncaster winners, must have been excited to see the pride of her stable, Grand Armee, bound clear of the field. It was all over. Or was it?

My hands were steering but I don't recall thinking about what needed to be done. After the checks Private Steer had copped and the effort required to get back into the race I had to save ground, stay calm, not use her up. That's what I had to do but I didn't have to think about it. My hands had instinctively taken Private Steer from the outside back to the inside – the shortest way home.

The brain is an amazing tool; it can cope with so much. It was already doing things like managing balance, sight, hearing, judgement of pace and now, with no effort, it was finding us a way through this maze of galloping horseflesh. We passed horse after horse, cutting through them, magically finding the runs just as we needed them. Then I saw Grand Armee in front. The race reports would suggest that it was a close-run thing but, at the 200-metre mark, I knew we were going to win. I knew Private Steer had the sectionals to overcome what had happened. She didn't falter in that amazing charge to the line.

Later, I would tell reporters it was the most incredible ride I had ever experienced – mindblowing. The fans were simply going off their heads, screaming, whooping, shouting. I took her back down the straight to shout and whoop it up with them. The celebrations went on and on. I wanted the fans to know just how much winning a Group 1 race in that fashion meant to me.

It almost seemed impossible to imagine that Private Steer could top that Doncaster effort. But, just five days later, we lined up again at Randwick, this time in the Group 1 weight-for-age All-Aged Stakes over 1400 metres. Many race goers viewed her charge from last to first in the Doncaster as little short of a miracle. But under handicap conditions the filly was obliged to carry no more than 53 kilograms. The weight-for-age conditions of the All-Aged, where she was up against an even classier field, would take away that advantage.

In so many respects the race was a replay the Doncaster. Once again, we found ourselves back in last place, sitting patiently, aiming to judge the pace to perfection knowing that this time we had 200 metres less to run. When the field banked into the straight and started to pan across the track, my instinct again was to take the shortest way home. The inside running offered inferior ground but there was no other option. Besides, Private Steer was one of those horses capable of rising above any difficulty, including losing a shoe in running the All-Aged. As the others fanned out across the track, I pulled her towards the inside rail and pinched a couple of lengths by cutting the corner. By then, her supporters who had backed her to start a 2–1 favourite must have been tearing their hair out. The stable silks were blue emblazoned with a gold lightning flash. Surely, the punters would have been muttering, lightning can't strike twice in the same week at Randwick.

Strike twice it did. Like a heavenly bolt she shot down that famous Randwick straight and simply burned some of the best weight-for-age performers in the land. Once again, there was absolutely nothing to spare as we grabbed Our Egyptian Raine on the line to win by a long neck, with Defier in third place. Private Steer's winning time of 1:21:61 was just half a second outside the course record.

The effort almost defied belief and Randwick was rocking like an old school bus as the fans realised they had witnessed one of racing's rare deeds. By then, the punters had come to expect a bit of post-race jubilation from the jockey. As we returned to scale, I leaped to my feet and rode Private Steer like a surfboard all the way to the winner's stall. There was still plenty of the laconic Aussie bushie in John O'Shea and he was happy to leave the celebrating to me. The trainer knew his horse and had been confident all along that she would back up after the Doncaster victory. She had taken her race winnings to $3.25 million from 18 starts and would head for a well-deserved spell, with the idea of preparing her for the Cox Plate at Moonee Valley in the spring.

That final day at the 2004 Easter carnival brought the most magical week of my life to a close. In four days of racing at Royal Randwick I had ridden no less than nine winners, five of them being Group 1 successes. It was almost inconceivable. That week proved to me that I had truly stepped away from my past and found a new, more positive way to prepare for the big events of the career I had chosen as a boy. The victories were wonderful, but not nearly as precious as the lessons I would take with me from a week in which I had been blessed with wonderful horses.

There would be plenty of rave reviews for my performance, but how could I explain it? Could I tell the media that I had become a big believer in the benefits of tapping into the psyche and harnessing that instinctive power of the brain? How could I explain that after the accident my whole life had taken a 180-degree turn? Could I stand at the microphone during the presentation and tell them that what Glen Boss does isn't important? For instance, how can you compare what I do with the struggles of a kid faced with a life-threatening illness? I have a terrific lifestyle, gorgeous wife, great kids and a beautiful home. What do I have to worry about compared to that kid's family? You have to keep things in perspective. All I had done was fall off a horse in Macau and, a few months later, a different Glen Boss had climbed back on.

In all, season 2003–04 would deliver a total of 10 Group 1 winners, twice as many as my previous best. This golden run was rounded out at the Brisbane winter carnival when Star Shiraz scored in the Sires' Produce Stakes. Right then, it seemed greedy to think that racing might deliver even greater fortune. But the party had just begun.

The clue to my destiny and what place I would ultimately claim in the history of Australian racing was tied up with a horse I had ridden in 2003–04. In fact, she had contributed to two of those 10 Group 1 victories. The sharper reader will have already spotted that, in the preceding passages, I have deliberately omitted mention of her, the reason being that this galloper deserves a separate story all of her own. Her name?

Makybe Diva.

14

When one door closes . . .

It was a Tuesday morning, 2 September, the second day of spring 2003. A regulation track gallop. Republic Lass felt as good as ever. I had that inescapable feeling of being up on top of a good horse. She had that definable difference – the special ingredient that sets the great Group 1 winners apart from the rest. Even at three-quarter pace, The Lass oozed star quality. Travelling over the Warwick Farm crossing I sensed she changed gait. It was just a flicker, a momentary thing, a tiny fluctuation in the rhythm, one hoof not coming down when it was supposed to. It pushed an alarm in my head. I conveyed the news to the mare's trainer Guy Walter and he said he would have her examined once she had cooled down. On the drive home from track work, I kept telling myself it was nothing, but still feared the worst. Later, the phone rang. It was Guy.

'She's bowed a tendon and we're going to retire her,' he said. Simple as that. Some trainers will break the bank to return a horse to racing health. Not Guy. He was always the absolute realist. Why put a noble animal through the grief of surgery and protracted treatment with no guarantee of a worthwhile outcome? Let her go to the paddock and rest. Start a new life as a great brood mare.

After 23 starts, which included victories in the AJC Australian Oaks and the Ranvet Stakes, the lustrous career of the brilliant galloper by Canny Lad out of the American mare Swift Seasons was abruptly ended.

My attitude has always been 'when one door closes, another one opens'. But this door was Republic Lass. Not an easy one to turn your back on. For ages I had been convinced she was destined to be the superstar of the spring of 2003; a galloper capable of winning the big ones – Cox Plates, Caulfield Cups and, yes, Melbourne Cups. When she had won the AJC Oaks as a three-year-old, her sectional times had been brilliant. But as she matured, she became a more grinding style of runner, indicating that she definitely had the ability to stay. She looked and felt like a Melbourne Cup winner in the making. The Lass had been the motivation that drove my recovery after breaking my neck. The thought of missing out on partnering her had driven me every step of the way through the post-fall trauma and painful rehabilitation. And now she was gone.

By its very nature, racing is a game that rarely looks back. The winning post is that way. In front of you. Never behind. The Lass was on her way to the retirement paddock and I had to re-examine my options. Pronto. It was early September. Spring was already underway. There was not a minute to waste.

The distinguished Flemington-based trainer David Hall had a couple of handy ones heading towards the cups so I gave him a call. I had ridden Pentastic for him before and knew he was a proven weight-for-age horse with great staying ability. 'Republic Lass has broken down,' I told David. 'Is there any chance I can ride Pentastic?' David's response was that he would stick with Steven Arnold on the basis that he could ride at 55 kilograms, the weight Pentastic would carry in the Melbourne Cup, as well as the weight-for-ages races. But then came the words that would define one of life's great forks in the road. 'There is this other one,' said David. 'A mare, Makybe Diva. In fact, I have a feeling she just might turn out to be the better of the two.'

I certainly knew of the horse. In 2002 she had won five in a row, including the Werribee Cup and the Group 2 Queen Elizabeth Stakes at Flemington. Like many potentially great stayers, she was a late bloomer. After being foaled in March 1999, she didn't have her first race until July 2002. Luke Currie had been her regular rider and had done a great job. Two months or so out from the 2003 spring carnival, she was no better than a 20–1 shot for the Melbourne Cup. But David's words had struck a chord in me. I didn't hesitate.

David Hall spoke to the mare's owner Tony Santic and they agreed that I would ride her in the Caulfield and Melbourne Cups while Luke would remain on her in the lead-up races. She didn't win, but I was impressed by the way she kept punching home. Meantime, her Cup price continued to shorten. As September warmed into October, David, Tony and I kept in constant touch, monitoring her progress and comparing notes.

By 2003, my routine for the spring carnival involved moving to Melbourne for six weeks. The strategy was to arrive in early October and remain in the Victorian capital until almost mid-November. So it was the Tuesday before the Caulfield Cup, one typically crisp spring morning at Flemington, when I first rode Makybe Diva. Prior to that, I could recollect having seen her in action the previous spring in track work when she won the Queen Elizabeth, but I hadn't taken too much notice.

My initial impression on seeing this well-bred bay thoroughbred up close was that she was still a relatively lightweight mare. She wasn't carrying a lot of condition and would have weighed no more than 460 kilograms.

The other thing I noticed as I walked her out was her demeanour. New rider or not, she had a lovely casual approach to it all, totally non-plussed about everything. Whatever way you pointed her she would respond without the slightest fuss or hesitation. But her most impressive characteristics began to show once I galloped her. The action was totally fluent, very efficient with no energy loss. David had deliberately left her a little underdone heading into the Caulfield Cup, knowing that the gruelling Melbourne Cup lay ahead. Consequently, on this morning he wanted me to give her a searching gallop. We went over a mile and a quarter in pretty slick time. I pulled her up and turned for the two- or three-minute walk back to the hut and within 30 seconds it was like she had never even exerted herself at all. Amazingly, her breathing had returned to near normal. On almost any other horse you can feel the beat of the great heart pulsing up through the saddle, such is the level of exertion and what the cardiovascular system needs to do to recover. But this time it was completely different. The mare's recovery rate was absolutely extraordinary. And she was still significantly short of peak fitness. With rising excitement I immediately conveyed my thoughts to her trainer.

'I've never ridden a horse with a recovery rate like this,' I reported. 'It's freakish.'

'Yeah, she's very clean-winded,' David affirmed.

'Clean-winded? Holy smoke, she must have massive lung capacity!'

On dismounting, I looked at her anew and noted how long-barrelled she was behind the girth. Later, sharp-eyed horsemen would point out her deep girth as a great indicator of a superior heart-lung capacity. Great lungs, good wind pipes, clean winded. She was long in the legs and rein – a real athlete – but her hindquarters were all muscle. Remember, this was our first encounter. I was blown away. The mare and I worked together again on the Thursday, just a steady session, and all my first impressions were re-affirmed.

Talking it over with David, I told him that I had never ridden one of the European-style classic stayers, the great ground-swallowing endurance horses with the sort of super-charged lung capacity that creates the impression that they could run all day. But, there was something about Makybe Diva that made me suspect she had something of that quality about her, plus a little extra of her own.

She drew very wide for the Caulfield Cup, one of the tough-est 2400-metre handicap events in the racing world. With the eventual winner Mummify showing the way, they were absolutely dawdling. The mare, from her wide position, tacked on in last place. We knew she was short of peak fitness and the distance, let alone the quality of the opposition, would be test-ing enough. But what I hadn't budgeted on was her winning desire. In the straight she simply went after them. With each massive stride her Melbourne Cup price was sent tumbling as she charged down the outside with an unbelievable run. Such was her speed over the latter stages of the race, her sectionals were right off the charts. To be able to stay is one thing, but to have such a blinding sprint to call on at the end of an endurance contest is simply astonishing. It was the perfect Melbourne Cup trial.

Riding her in track work had been impressive. But it is not until you get a thoroughbred under true race conditions that you really find out what it is made of. By the time I brought her back to the enclosure after the Caulfield Cup her amazing recovery rate had returned her breathing to normal. It was like she could have gone out and run the race again. Given the state of her preparation, nobody could have expected her to turn in such a performance. By any rights she should not have been capable of doing what she did that day. If she had run home sweetly, got to the furlong and knocked up to finish in the first eight, it would have been more than a worthy effort and indicated she was still on an upward curve heading into the Melbourne Cup. Instead, she amazed me by running a second quicker over the final 600 metres than I ever imagined she could. There and then I was already prepared to admit to myself she was the best horse I had ever ridden. She was a rare breed indeed.

Chance is a fine thing. Republic Lass's exit had been heartbreaking. But, and this was hard to admit, here was another mare whose ability would certainly have eclipsed The Lass in the spring of 2003. No matter whether the tempo of a race is fast, even or slow, few horses have what it takes to jump out and relax, conserve energy and, when you ask for an effort, deliver in a way that simply defies belief. The Diva had that ability. At that point, although I had never been on the winner in Australia's greatest race, I was prepared to make a declaration to myself and Makybe Diva's connections: 'She'll win the Melbourne Cup.'

One characteristic that I had already identified in Makybe Diva was her ability to exceed what she had been prepared for. For example, if you prepared her for 1600 metres she could run 2000 or 2400. She didn't need work. The risk with her was that you might over-train her and she would lose her sprint, that incredible burst she offered at the end of a race. Without that sprint she was just another plugging stayer. So it was important that we trained her for something like 400 metres less than what she would have to run. Her ability to come off a light workload and then run a gruelling distance race is something that I had never seen in all my time around thoroughbreds.

Between the Caulfield Cup and the first Tuesday in November, Melbourne Cup day, she continued to work steadily with me aboard on the fast days of track work at Flemington. For many Cup horses, the Mackinnon Stakes at Flemington on the Saturday is an essential part of the build-up, the last serious hit-out before the big one. However, we decided not to start her in the Mackinnon. After the Caulfield Cup, David sought my opinion about running her on the Saturday before the Melbourne Cup. My view was that it might take the freshness out of her. Here was a horse who thrived on being slightly underdone. My response must have confirmed what he was already thinking and Tony was more than happy with the qualified advice.

On the Friday, David phoned to tell me to be at Werribee at five o'clock on the Saturday morning. The Werribee Cup had been held that week and the course was in great shape. So instead of running her in the Mackinnon that afternoon, we gave her a workout early in the morning away from prying eyes and the pressure of Flemington. I took her over 2000 metres at a pretty solid tempo, going about 12.5–13 seconds per furlong. It was a solid gallop. Then I clicked it up a notch and she breezed the final 600 in about 34 seconds. I couldn't hold her, she was going that quick. After the gallop, I just let her go for another half a lap to make sure she was spot on. Again, 30 seconds after I pulled her up and started walking her back she was totally relaxed, breathing normally. A searching gallop was just a stroll in the park for her. She put her head down and had a pick at the grass as if to say, 'Call that a workout? That was nothing!'

There was a lone clocker in attendance and he was looking at his timepiece shaking his head in disbelief.

The nervous owner had come down with some members of his family to watch her work. I joined Tony and David to declare: 'If she is as good on Tuesday as she is today, she will win it. Nothing will beat her.'

I told Tony he could bet with confidence.

Left: My first horse was a painted pony called Pride. Together we competed in many events at Gympie Pony Club.

Below: Everyone was happy when I won my first important race at the Gympie races in 1986. Even the horse, Ala Giant, is smiling.

Sloane and me at the 1993 Golden Slipper dinner, shortly after our arrival in Sydney.

NEWSPIX

An astounding sprint by Telesto (right) carried us past the post in the 1994 Chipping Norton Stakes at Warwick Farm, giving me my first Group 1 victory.

The reception by the crowd following my win on Flying Spur in the 1995 Golden Slipper was like nothing I'd ever experienced. This against-the-odds victory was a turning point in my career and took me to a new level.

Sprint By, seen here after winning the Gosford Cup in 1995, is one of my all-time favourite horses. With the exception of two races, I rode him for his entire career.

Despite drawing a bad barrier and not starting well, Sky Heights won the Yalumba Stakes in 2000 in a real show of courage.

I rode Shogun Lodge in the 2002 Doncaster (right), coming second behind the magnificent Sunline (left, ridden by Greg Childs).

Left: It's a fine line between flying on a thoroughbred and falling off. Accidents are an unfortunate part of racing, like this fall I suffered during track work when the horse threw me off.

Below: Carter (middle) and Tayte (right) helped keep my spirits up following my disastrous fall in Macau in 2002. Here I'm wearing the barbaric-looking halo brace that kept my head and neck stable while the fractures in my neck healed.

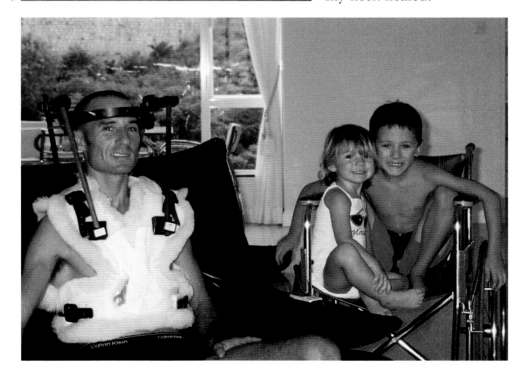

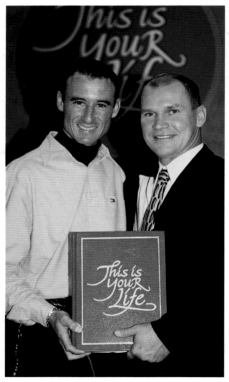

I've learned the value of the saying 'Your mates are your mates.' My mate Billy Cross is the most humble and down-to-earth bloke you could ever meet (*above left*). Scott Perrin has a way of making business sound as exciting as horse racing (*above right*), and as a card-carrying member of the little bloke's brigade, I'm in awe of Allan Langer's skill and courage (*below left*).

Sloane and I sit with John Brown (centre), Lucy Stanton (right) and Bob Stanton (far right), who all offered me tremendous support following my fall in Macau.

You can see the relief on my face at winning the Toorak Handicap on Shot Of Thunder in October 2002. Only four months earlier I was lying on a sodden racetrack in Macau with a broken neck.

The wins kept coming, and what a choice Choisir turned out to be. He carried me to victory in the Lightning Stakes in February 2003, and went on to set a track record at Royal Ascot.

NEWSPIX/CRAIG HUGHES

SPORT THE LIBRARY

I owe plenty to the amazing filly Republic Lass. Here she's leading the field in the AJC Oaks in April 2002, and in 2003 she held off the great Northerly to win the Ranvet Stakes.

Starcraft, winning here at Rosehill Gardens, is one of the best horses I've ever ridden – a giant of a stallion.

Private Steer's victory in the 2004 Doncaster will go down as one of the best of all time. She came from an impossible position (left) to beat Grand Armee (far right) and Ambulance (centre) soundly.

NEWSPIX/KELLY BARNES

Fastnet Rock (right) was all class, but though we had a glimpse of his greatness, we never saw the best of him.

Sloane and me at our wedding in Port Douglas in 2004. Carter (middle flower girl) and Tayte were joined by Mattie and Charlie Brown, family friends.

The start
of a legend:
Makybe Diva
in action in
the 2003
Melbourne
Cup.

What a magnificent sight. The Diva (centre) took the lead in the home
straight to win the 2004 Melbourne Cup, setting Flemington alight
despite the gloomy conditions.

You can hardly see the Diva for her crowd of admirers following the Cox Plate in 2005.

Above: Nothing will ever replicate the feeling I experienced as the mighty Makybe Diva galloped into immortality on Tuesday 1 November 2005.

Left: While the Diva looked on, I jumped straight into the arms of her owner, Tony Santic, following her victory in the 2005 Melbourne Cup.

Sloane, who had supported me for so long, knew exactly how I felt after the Diva's historic third Cup win.

The Diva's owner, Tony Santic (left), and trainer, Lee Freedman (right), join me in raising her Melbourne Cup trophies in celebration.

Diva believers turned out in force for a celebratory parade in Port Lincoln. Lee Freedman (right) helps me show off her winnings.

What a way to avoid the traffic! I'd recently earned my licence, and relished the opportunity to fly myself from home to Randwick for Doncaster Day, 2006.

In 2006 I did a two-month stint racing in Japan. Carter and Tayte enjoyed our visit to Tokyo Disneyland.

While my commitment to racing and my career is solid, family will always come first. My memories of racing wins are that much sweeter because they were along with me for the ride.

15

The Makybe Cup

Tuesday couldn't come quick enough.

On the Monday afternoon we gathered at the Hall stables to finalise our strategy for the race. We went through the field, evaluated the barrier draw and talked about the possible dangers. Makybe Diva had drawn 14 which was fine by me – I was more interested in what sort of pace would be on because that would determine where we needed to be during the run. My thinking was to be outside the first 10 horses and inside the next 18. Fence or rail, it wouldn't matter. We knew she would come off the mark with speed and would do a 34.5 for the final 600 metres, which no other horse is capable of at the end of a 3200-metre run. That ability to accelerate in the closing stages meant I could make up many lengths in very rapid time. If I positioned her correctly during the run, and she peeled off that sprint, she should win. Our strategy was locked in. Almost. The trainer had a final directive.

'There is one thing I want you to do,' David said. 'When you get to the 600-metre mark, I want you to count to 10 before you release the brakes.'

The importance of not being impatient was already in my head, but once David emphasised it, the strategy was there to stay. I would time the run so that she was peaking at the 200, or even 100, but not the 300-metre mark.

David's trust in me and his practice of encouraging my input had been very gratifying. I especially appreciated the 'team' concept – trainer, owner and jockey – working together to shape a strategy to snatch the greatest turf prize on offer in Australasia.

It was an unlikely team: the blue-chip trainer in David Hall, a consummate horseman born and bred into a family of thoroughbred trainers; the kid from Caboolture who had literally broken his neck pursuing his dreams, and, perhaps the most interesting of the lot, the tuna fishing tycoon, Tony Santic.

Born on Lastovo, one of the hundreds of islands fringing the coast of Croatia in the Adriatic Sea, Tony had arrived in Australia in 1958 as a six-year-old. His family landed in Geelong but, heeding the call of their fishing heritage, moved to Port Lincoln to establish a life in commercial fishing. As a young man Tony had chased the orange roughie in the cold waters off the southern mainland and around the wild coastline of Tasmania before staking a claim in the Port Lincoln tuna industry. Reduction in tuna quotas sent some businesses broke and others to the brink, but Tony managed to fend off the banks and bailiffs to stay afloat. As a young father of five, he had no other option. Those tough times made him a smarter operator and he would ultimately earn a reputation as one of the most progressive and innovative figures in the tuna business. The eventual introduction of tuna farming put the industry on a new economic footing. Bold initiatives in large-scale refrigeration storage helped establish the Santics' company Tuna International as the second biggest in Port Lincoln.

All the hard work, high risk and smart thinking paid off. By the late 1990s, Tony was one seriously wealthy fisherman. To that point, racing had been a hobby, something to do with his spare cash and whatever time he could afford away from work. Now, it was time to put it on a serious footing. He went to New Zealand supposedly to buy a good mare. Instead, he came back with 30 horses, the makings of a serious racing and breeding business. Soon, his racing silks – royal blue with white stars and red and white checks, the colours of his country of birth – were a fixture around the tracks of South Australia and Victoria. In 1997, he appointed David Hall as his principal trainer.

I had worn Tony's colours once or twice before and therein lies a tale that would shape the course of our long-term relationship. Tony had never led in a Group 1 winner but, with yours truly in the saddle on Royal Code, it looked like his luck was about to change. It was the Australian Guineas at Flemington and, with Royal Code being a colt, it was a very important race for his future stud prospects. Royal Code was favourite and the stable had reason to be very confident, providing the jockey did his job. Instead, I blundered. Never before had I dropped the whip during the course of a race. But on this particular day, the persuader and the jockey somehow parted company. It would not have been a problem but for the fact that my ride took his mind off the job in the last half furlong. A couple of taps with the whip would have restored the concentration. I felt for the whip and it wasn't there. I don't even remember fumbling – my hand simply came up empty. I had to resort to riding him hands and heels as hard as I could. We placed second. A sure thing and what would have been Tony's first Group 1 success went begging. It can be career suicide for a jockey to admit to such a fundamental error. I'm sure any number of riders would have come up with an excuse as to how the whip came adrift. Instead, at the post-mortem between myself, trainer David Hall and owner, I said, 'It was my fault. I dropped the whip. I'm sorry. I've just cost you a Group 1.'

Tony put his hand on my shoulder and said, 'There will be another race.'

I couldn't believe it. My fumble had probably cost him millions in stud prospects for the colt. Not many blokes in the cutthroat world of racing would have dealt with it in such a way.

Much later, Tony would tell me: 'If you had come up with any other excuse or told a lie, you would never have ridden for me again.'

They say truth is beauty. I lived to fight another day for Tony Santic and ride his beautiful mare Makybe Diva.

Like her owner, The Diva was an import who had arrived downunder at a very tender age. Her dam Tugela was in foal to Desert King when agent John Foote bought her for Tony at a bloodstock sale in England. When Tugela foaled at Britton House Stud in March 1999, the qualified advice was to transport the mare but leave the foal behind. The reasoning was that the seasonal differences between the Northern and Southern Hemispheres meant the youngster would be giving away six months start to her future racing rivals. Surprisingly, she was unwanted when offered for sale at Newmarket auction, failing even to meet the reserve price. So the mare arrived in Australia with her foal at foot. It's easy to be wise after the event. Five years later, Tugela was covered by the star stallion Redoute's Choice to produce a colt which sold for $2.5 million at Sydney's Easter sale.

The lack of auction interest in the filly was hard to fathom. She had champions on both sides of her bloodlines. Tugela, a dual Group 1 winner in France, was the daughter of Riverman, the two-time French champion sire. Her grand-dam's sire, Roberto, was not only an English Derby winner but the sire of the Melbourne Cup winner At Talaq. Other winners in her lineage were Katsura by Northern Dancer, a five-time champion sire in England and the United States, and mare Noble Fancy by two-time United Kingdom champion sire and Prix de l'Arc de Triomphe winner Vaguely Noble. The Diva's sire, Desert King, won the Irish Derby and became a leading sire of outstanding gallopers with staying ability. And his sire was the mighty Danehill, creator of a worldwide dynasty of thorough-bred champions.

The yearling was sent to horse country near the Upper Hunter township of Scone to be broken in and educated by one of the best, Greg Bennett. I have no doubt that her genes played a big part in giving her such a magnificent heart-lung system, but so did the early work she received under Greg's tutelage. He galloped her on the steep hill country outside Scone and knew by the way she handled the tough uphill going that she was something special. With that sort of education to fall back on, The Diva would find the Flemington straight a bit of a cakewalk.

Greg would later tell reporters that his team had broken in plenty of good horses and that the best of them give off a special quality. Makybe Diva had that quality and Greg knew the filly was destined for a wonderful career. How wonderful? Only time would tell. I suspect she had a lovely disposition as a yearling and credit goes to the breaker for preserving that quality throughout her education. When Greg Bennett had completed his assignment Makybe Diva must have been an impressive package: tractable but spirited, athletic and courageous.

The job of training the imported filly was eventually assigned to Tony's principal trainer, David Hall. The task of naming her fell to the staff at Tony's Port Lincoln office. Maureen Dellar, Kylie Bascomb, Belinda Groske, Dianne Tonkin and Vanessa Parthenis took the first two letters of each of their first names and banged them together. Makybe Diva.

The Melbourne Cup is the greatest prize in Australasian racing. For too long it had figured as the most obvious and painful gap in my trophy cabinet. My relationship with the great race had not been a happy one. Karasi had carried me into fourth place in 2001. A year later I was close but not close enough with a fifth on Pentastic. But the greatest disappointment of all occurred in 1998 when I rode the brilliant mare Champagne. Three days before, with Greg Hall aboard, she had devastated the Mackinnon field and looked ripe for the big race on the Tuesday. I gave her a beautiful ride, she sprinted early and quickly and was so strong in the run home that the race looked all over. Then, just a few strides from the post, she faltered and we were passed by the fast-finishing Jezabeel. Champagne never raced again. I don't know what happened to her that day but my guess is that her slashing effort in the Mackinnon had taken too much out of her.

Top jockeys can campaign for decades and ride countless

winners but still head into retirement without the most prized trophy of them all. George Moore, rated alongside Neville Sellwood as Australia's greatest jockey, rode 2278 winners at home and overseas but hung up his riding whip never having won a Melbourne Cup.

In 2003, the first Tuesday of November couldn't come quickly enough. My view was that only a monumental slice of bad luck could stop us winning the Cup.

Race day dawned on a beautiful Melbourne spring Tuesday as a Cup record crowd of 122,736 found its way to Flemington. The problem with being on a good thing is that outside of winning in style, all you can do is blow it. Both David and Tony were as nervous as a couple of young grooms on their wedding day. By then, I had been on the mare enough for her to know the sound of my voice and to recognise my touch. One reassuring word and I could feel her relax underneath me. This one was no temperamental diva. On her big day she paraded in her usual nonchalant way. With 51 kilograms on her back, the mare cantered down to the barrier in her easy-going way, ears flopping, totally relaxed. Neither the occasion nor the crowd was going to upset her routine.

For a stayer, she would always have incredible gate speed. Take a snapshot of the horses leaving the barrier and she would often be one of the first out and racing. One second she would be standing there so quiet and then, bang, she would explode. I put it down to her incredible power, particularly in her hindquarters.

We came out of the gate in great shape and in no time had locked into the race plan – outside the first eight horses and inside the first 18. Exactly where we wanted to be. The tempo was even and she was just jogging along doing her thing. At about the 1400-metre mark a horse immediately in front came back on us and she threw her head up. But that was for no more than a few strides. We slowed as the field bunched momentarily, and then she slipped straight back into her familiar relaxed mode.

It was a great place to be. The Diva was so calm, it felt like we were entering 'The Zone'. Flemington would have been thrumming like a power station, energised by the sheer weight of interest in the race that stops the nation. The pounding of hooves from a full Cup field would have sounded like thunder. But, here we were, seemingly becalmed in the eye of the hurricane. All had gone quiet.

I was aware that horses outside us were working hard, looking to go forward close to the 1000-metre mark. But where we were, nothing disturbed my sense of serenity. Surely, this was 'The Zone'.

The farther we went, the more I sensed a powerful spring was coiling beneath me. The Diva's racing experience and her thoroughbred instincts told her that she would soon be called upon for a huge effort. She was gathering herself. All around us, other horses were making their moves. Her competitive instinct was to go with them, but she had a jockey on board who was holding her up. 'Patience, patience,' I whispered. Her internal coil tightened on itself. It felt like she was set to explode. Then we were bounding past the 600, and, like a monk silently uttering his mantra, I began the count 'One, two . . .'

Horses slowing at the front were coming back to us while those making their runs had swept wide.

'Five, six . . .' We might have been closer to the lead but now there were more gallopers in front us than at any time in the race. Ahead, I could see other jockeys starting to panic as they fought for a clear run. Aboard The Diva, I was at ease. She had worked her way up towards the leaders with no effort at all and I almost giggled with delight knowing how much horse I had underneath me with little more than 400 metres to run. With absolute certainty I knew she would run about 22.5 seconds in the final 400 metres and nothing could catch her. The risk on a conventional stayer in the Cup is having your chances ruined by being blocked for a run. But I knew the mare's devastating sprint could get us out of trouble even if we didn't get clear until the 200-metre mark.

From the 700 to the 400-metre mark the runs had kept coming for us as we sliced our way through two-thirds of the field. As each horse in front moved out looking for a run, I would take that spot. At the 300-metre mark she exploded. Within a few bounds Makybe Diva was going at twice the speed of her opponents as her withering sprint swept us past fading horses and we closed on the leaders. Throughout her racing career, no horse had ever passed Makybe Diva in the straight. On this day, of all days, she wasn't about to relinquish that record.

The Cup was ours!

While Flemington erupted all around us, I was experiencing a sensation never before encountered in my riding career. The Australian racing calendar is crammed with great races like the Doncaster and the Cox Plate, but everything pales along-side the Melbourne Cup. From the dyed-in-the-wool devotee to the once-a-year punter, the Cup is the greatest race of them all – the event that stops a nation. For every owner, trainer and jockey it is the ultimate aim. From the time young jockeys first enter the stable, it's all they have been dreaming about. When The Diva swept to victory, all the hard work, every bit of training and sacrifice, all the early mornings, fitness sessions, setbacks, injuries and sheer persistence came together in one mind-blowing moment of release. It was almost an out-of-body experience, such as I'd never felt.

In previous years, I'd looked on as the media had asked the winning jockey how it felt to win the Melbourne Cup. Let me tell you how it feels: it's like an athlete has invested 15 years of training and tuition knowing that winning the Olympic 100-metres sprint final comes down to mere seconds. The athlete rises perfectly off the blocks, gets into an ideal stride and then powers on to break the tape. Of course, it is never really about just those 10 seconds – it is about the 15 years invested in the effort. Once you cross that line every sinew in your body that has been on hold for every moment of those long years lets loose in a massive release. It's like a giant valve has been opened.

The closest feeling I can relate it to is what you experience when watching your child being born. Standing up in the irons, I felt the tide of emotion tingle through my toes and all the way up through my body, bringing me to tears of utter ecstasy. How does it feel to win the Melbourne Cup? Now I knew.

By now, the Glen Boss Group 1 celebration was starting to become a signature event. But this was a Melbourne Cup so I cranked it up a notch or three on the way back to the enclosure. As for Makybe Diva, she was again showing why nothing could catch her in the staying stakes. A few minutes before she had been a great locomotive steaming full tilt towards the finish post. Now, just minutes after the effort, she was breathing easily as her amazing cardiovascular system eased to a gentle simmer.

When the celebrations and presentations were done, I would be sustained by an inner glow that lingered long into the night and all through the ensuing week. It was the sense of a job well done. From the outset, the 2003 Cup campaign had been a team effort between trainer and jockey with the owner placing his total faith in our judgement. I consider David Hall not just a wonderful trainer but a great mate and, right from the start, he had welcomed my input. We had hatched a plan and worked on it to the smallest degree, seeking to identify and eliminate any risk that might prevent the mare performing to her potential. Yet, racing is such a fluky game that it is extremely rare for a plan to work to the absolute letter. In a heartbeat, things can change and months of planning will fly out the window. The raw statistics underline just how crucial a role the detailed planning played in the Cup win. Although she was the best staying mare in Australia, carried only 51 kilograms and no rival could match her sectional times, yet, at the end of a perfect preparation and a beautiful run, she still won by no more than a length. One oversight in our strategy, one tiny flaw in the plan, might have been enough to reduce that margin. Yes, it was extremely gratifying knowing that between us and the mare, we had got it absolutely right.

16
Again?

A mid all the euphoria and celebrations, the planning was already underway to have another crack at the Cup. Since the race was first run in 1861, Peter Pan, Rain Lover and Think Big were the only winners to have their names inscribed twice. None of them were mares. We were convinced The Diva had the potential to be the first mare to go back to back. By November 2004, Makybe Diva would be six years old and still in her prime. The patience of Tony Santic in waiting for the mare to mature before starting her racing career meant she still had plenty of great runs left in her. The experience of 2003 indicated we had figured out a winning formula. If she remained sound and we could start her in spring on the back of a similar preparation, her chances looked more than promising.

While Makybe Diva headed for a well-earned spell after her Cup heroics, we planned to bring her back for a reasonably light autumn concentrating on a weight-for-age campaign before setting her up for the following spring.

However, at her first Group 1 start back from the spell a flint-hard Flemington, suffering under southern Australia's protracted drought, brought her undone in the Australian Cup. If this seemingly bulletproof mare did have an Achilles heel, it was hard tracks. She always had soft heels and they would bruise easily, causing her great pain and discomfort. But such was her courage and winning desire, she would always attempt to gallop through the pain barrier. Rather than discounting her, it only increased my admiration for this exceptional horse. Nonetheless, the rock-hard surfaces made for a less-than-ideal preparation for the autumn of 2004.

The plan was to take her to Sydney to run in the Ranvet Stakes at what would be her first start in the clockwise direction. Once again, she struck a surface as hard as bitumen, was obviously a little distracted and turned in an average performance. Suspecting that she was having trouble concentrating in a race, the decision was made to run her in blinkers. We believed that the races ahead would be slow-run affairs in which it was easy for a horse of her ability to lose focus. So, as well as the blinkers, the strategy was to put a bit of speed on early, get her up on the tempo and be in a position to strike when the speed was on. In the Ranvet, I had ridden her outside the leader but once they kicked for home, that scorching Diva acceleration was missing. In that autumn she struck four hard tracks in a row, including the BMW Stakes at Rosehill, and appeared a shadow of her former self. There was no power going forward. The pain in her heels just made her want to run sideways. Track regulars were scratching their chins and speculating that she may be nothing more than a good 3200-metre horse, that she simply didn't have the speed to handle anything up to 2400 metres.

The Diva had been nominated for the Sydney Cup. Instead, with her autumn campaign in tatters, she was sent home to Melbourne. But then it rained in Sydney. I rang David to ask what he had planned for the mare.

'It's raining in Sydney,' I told him. 'She'll get a soft track for the Sydney Cup.'

David put her straight back on the float. She had been trained to run a mile-and-a-half in the BMW, so she was always going to be fit enough for the two miles of the Sydney Cup. The question was: would we see the true Diva, the champion of the previous spring?

Our prayers were soon answered. The instant she put one foot down on the softer going, it was apparent she was back. I was having a brilliant autumn carnival in 2004, and the return of The Diva made it that much sweeter. With 55 kilograms on her back, she cantered out at Randwick on a track officially described as 'good' and charged from behind on the inside rail to become the first horse in 38 years to win the Melbourne–Sydney cups double. 'That's more like it,' I said to myself. Meanwhile, the doubters went right on thinking that she was exclusively a two-miler. They reckoned the Sydney Cup win over 3200 metres merely confirmed that impression. I knew otherwise. My conviction was that she could sprint. If her trainer had wanted to set her for a race like the Doncaster over 1600 metres, she would do it. The critics could think as they wished. I was beginning to understand her better and my admiration for her continued to grow. Sure, she preferred the softer going, but even when it was hard and painful, she still tried to do her best. She was always having a go. Here was a thoroughbred who would run through brick walls.

It wasn't long after the Sydney carnival that David Hall received a great compliment for his talent when presented with the opportunity to train in Hong Kong. His parting gift for Tony Santic and Makybe Diva would prove the ultimate making of the mare.

'I think we should send her down to Lee Freedman at Mornington,' David advised.

The Freedman team had established a brilliant set-up at their Markdel complex near Rye on the Mornington Peninsula. Compared with the restricted confines of Flemington where a thoroughbred can soon become bored with the same routine and sights, the training farm established by the Freedmans offered fresh country air, wide open spaces, a seaside environment and plenty of peace and quiet. David had seen the property and knew better than anybody that Lee was a brilliant trainer. He was convinced that the mare would thrive in such an environment, as opposed to remaining at Flemington where she would get stale. It was a masterstroke.

Lee Freedman: 'That change of scene came along at the right time for Makybe Diva. Horses can get bored. From the time the mare arrived it was obvious she was loving it. She definitely thrived.'

While Makybe Diva moved house to Mornington, my focus fell on the approaching winter carnival in Brisbane. However, my

recollection of the manoeuvrings was that Lee was a bit appre-
hensive about taking on The Diva. After all, she had won a
Melbourne Cup and lightning very rarely strikes twice. He
might have thought he was on a kick-in-the-bum-to-nothing.
However, he was of the opinion that it was better to have her
in his stable than racing against her. There was a period of
adjustment for everybody. Although Tony Santic had plenty
of horses racing throughout Victoria and South Australia, this
was his first association with the Freedmans. Sending his most
prized thoroughbred to another stable and having to establish
new lines of communication with a trainer he barely knew was
a considerable step. But Tony trusted David's call and did all
within his power to make the transition a smooth one.

As for me, I was in no doubt David had pulled the right rein
in recommending Lee.

The next time I saw the mare she was bigger, and stronger.
Like David, Lee is a wonderful conditioner of racehorses. The
Freedman trademark is that his horses get bigger and stronger
as they race. My understanding is that the relaxed environment
of Mornington where the horses are out in the yards on a daily
basis is perfect for allowing them to draw maximum benefit
from the Freedmans' conditioning program. The surrounds
were ideal for the mare. She was out in the paddock relaxing,
eating well and getting worked twice a day. It was a program
that suited her down to the ground.

The transformation was unbelievable. When I left The Diva
at the end of autumn, her racing weight would have been
around 480 kilograms. Three months later, when Lee invited
me down to Mornington to look her over, the mare was
well beyond 500 kilos and still growing. Her rear end was as
wide as a boardroom table – that would give her awesome

power – and she had the lungs and heart to go with it. Everything about her was right. At that point I realised she was on her way to being a superstar. She had always been a great racehorse but now she had evolved into a machine that would prove unstoppable.

Before David Hall left for Hong Kong, Lee had spent time with him doing the homework on Makybe Diva. Now it was my turn to fill in any of the gaps. I emphasised the importance of keeping her underdone. I wasn't sure what value he placed on that advice. It didn't matter – on Caulfield Cup day 2004, the mare would show us for herself.

Once again the focus was all about winning the Melbourne Cup. The Diva went into the spring with a similar preparation as the previous year: the 1600-metre of the Feehan Stakes at Moonee Valley in September, stepping up to the 2000 metres of the Turnbull Stakes at Flemington a month later, followed by the 2400 metres of the Caulfield Cup on 16 October. She finished a close second in the Feehan and came from a long way back to miss a placing in the Turnbull.

I arrived in Melbourne the week before to ride her in work leading up to the Caulfield Cup. She was as big as a house. Not just big, but also fat. Lee's plan was to run her at Caulfield and then tune her up for the Melbourne Cup. Carrying 55.5 kilograms, she was heading into one of the toughest handicap races on the calendar way underdone. At that stage, her price was about 15–1 and I told Tony that she was absolutely flying in training but I didn't think her condition was forward enough for her to win a race as formidable as the Caulfield Cup. Tony Santic never bets each way. He had $100,000 on her to win.

Lee's instructions to me were to look after her and make sure she finished strongly over the final 200 metres. We drew alley 22 and she was shuffled back to near last. The ultimate winner Elvstroem was having a whale of a time dawdling along with the leaders. For once, I couldn't navigate a way through the field, so we had to go wide. *Bang!* With that breathtaking burst of acceleration, she took off after the field, sweeping by some of her rivals as if they were standing still, until she caught Elvstroem. They waged a ding-dong battle to the post where The Diva went down by no more than a head. It was an incredible run. I thought this galloper had exhausted all her surprises but still she managed to amaze me. Given what I knew of her racing history and her condition, she should never have turned in such a performance. She had produced a four-length better effort than anybody could have expected of her.

We returned to the enclosure to find the normally unflappable Lee Freedman in what might have passed for a state of shock. He knew he hadn't prepared her for such a performance.

'I told you so,' I said. With an incredulous shake of his head, the hall-of-fame trainer indicated that he, too, had become a Diva believer.

We knew we were on a good thing and, from that point on, stuck to the basics of the plan that had worked so well the previous year. However, this year there would be no Mackinnon Stakes for The Diva. Instead, she would gallop on the Saturday morning before the Cup at the Mornington racetrack, not far from Lee's Markdel property, rather than Werribee. Instead of running on her own, she worked with a partner over 2000 metres on the course proper. The other horse went out about four lengths ahead. We trundled along behind at a good tempo.

Now, what I am about to tell you next explains my confidence about the mare's chances of winning her second Melbourne Cup.

With 200 metres to go, the other horse was six lengths in front. At the finishing post, Makybe Diva was four lengths clear. The clockers turned to each other in astonishment as if to say, 'Have you got the same time? This can't be right.' That one hard gallop on Caulfield Cup day had tuned her up. After that run I said to Lee: 'Just watch how much improvement she makes between now and the Melbourne Cup.' Her workload increased and she lifted. When the mare came into full fitness her coat dappled up and she absolutely glowed. Day by day she became more aggressive, stronger, a warhorse working her way up to a pitch. That was exactly how she looked on Mackinnon day, just three sleeps before the first Tuesday in November. She was perfect.

17

A muddied warrior

Cup day. Sloane was in Melbourne getting ready to join 98,000 race fans at the biggest party of the year – the Melbourne Cup. I can remember ringing her to say that, just like last year, the mare was ready. The entire stable was quietly confident. Tony wanted to put a packet on her but then he started thinking that the prize money was so huge he didn't need to have a bet. But he backed her anyway. Tony Santic had backed his judgement his entire life. On this day, of all days, he wasn't about to break the habit. If Tony had been disappointed at being pipped in the Caulfield Cup, in time he would be grateful the mare had run second. A win would have incurred a weight penalty of 2 kilos. By running second she copped no penalty, making it into the Melbourne Cup field with a very reasonable 55.5 kilograms on her back.

The previous year the mare had worn the number 12 saddlecloth and drew barrier 14. The rise in weight for 2004 saw her in the number five saddlecloth and this time she would be starting from barrier seven. I wasn't bothered where she started. Underneath me was a horse capable of overcoming just about any setback the Cup could throw at her. The only tiny crack of doubt in this otherwise perfect picture was a Flemington course which, although not rock hard, was certain to offer firm going.

Melbourne's ability to deliver four seasons in one day is legendary. But this time it outdid itself. The program was about halfway through when out of a perfect 25-degree spring day blew a howling, purple and black storm. It whipped through Flemington, turning umbrellas inside out and sending others spiralling skywards. Race books were snatched from hands, form guides sent flapping and thousands of carefully planned picnics reduced to a rain-sodden shambles as the weather roared across Flemington. A fortune's worth of millinery was ripped to tatters as scantily clad young things shivered in their drenched Cup fashions. The fortunate few found cover, but most of the crowd was exposed to the driving wind and rain.

As we paraded before the Cup, the thoroughbreds, acting on age-old instincts, tried to turn their rumps into the wind to shield themselves from the driving elements. It was hardly the picture postcard impression of a Cup parade but I didn't mind. Like a farmer celebrating the end of a long drought, I was ecstatic: the rain was coming down in such torrents that I knew the sting would definitely be taken out of the ground by the time Makybe Diva made it to the barrier. The race couldn't start quickly enough – and not just because I was on a good thing. The temperature had plummeted to 10 degrees and we were drenched to the skin in our silks, shivering from the cold. The sooner the action started, the quicker we would be warm again.

In the barrier, the mare was her usual unflappable self. The plan was to ride in a similar position as the previous year. However, with the wet conditions it was bound to be a bit more of a slugfest than last year. Lee Freedman never overloaded me with instructions, preferring to trust my experience and instincts to get the job done. Instead, he offered just one or two words of advice to reaffirm the strategy. 'Whatever you do,' he had said in the mounting yard, 'be in front at the 200, and don't get there too late.' He was absolutely right – if it became a slugfest, The Diva would just grind the other horses down; in a real ding-dong battle, she would be the last one standing.

We came out of the gate like a super-charged V8 leaving the grid – all power but still as smooth as butter. Amid the hurly-burly of the first furlong or so she soon found her rhythm, unbothered by the activity around her. Considering the wet conditions, the early pace was pretty brisk and on settling down I found we were a bit farther back in the field than the previous year and were affording the leaders a bit more than I wanted. Still, I wasn't worried. Beneath me, the mare was travelling effortlessly and I knew that no other galloper in the field could match her ability to accelerate and cover ground so quickly, especially in the soft going.

We were back on the fence, The Diva ticking over like a metronome conserving energy for when she would be required to give her all. Serene is not a word you would normally associate with the flurry and adrenalin of the great race but that's how it felt tucked away on the fence. Serene.

At the 1600-metre mark my internal computer went to work calibrating all the equations: race position, pace and par-ticularly how the big horse beneath me was travelling. All was perfect. There are a million ways to lose a race but approaching the 800 I was delighted. At that stage of the battle, no horse in the race could possibly have been travelling better than Makybe Diva. It was déjà vu – surely 2004 would be an absolute repeat of 2003. We were on our way to back-to-back victories in the Melbourne Cup!

No sooner had the thought entered my head than reality dragged me back to the moment. Immediately in front of us Delzao, on the fence, was rocking and rolling around like a rudderless battleship. Here was a problem presenting itself at the very point of the race when we needed to make ground very quickly. The briefest hold-up here could spell catastrophe. 'Where's he going?' I thought to myself as jockey Steven King battled to keep Delzao pointed in the right direction. The galloper rocked to the left and then swayed to the right, opening up the narrowest of gaps on the rail. Here was our chance and I didn't need a written invitation. I clicked the message to the mare. Whoosh! Like a cannonball she shot through that space at such speed that we almost took Steven's foot out of the iron and the paint off the fence. Later, Kingy and I would talk about that moment and he would shake his head in amazement at the memory of the mare's awesome acceleration as she went through the opening.

To those members of the TV audience who truly understand racing, it must have looked amazing. In a twinkling she had gone from an almost impossible position to leap right on to the hooves of the leaders. This was where I wanted to be. Now we had second race favourite Vinnie Roe in our sights, wide and in front. In the soft conditions the imported galloper with his staying credentials and ability to run the distance right out was definitely the one to beat. Approaching the turn, big Vinnie angled out looking for clear ground for the long surge down the

Flemington straight. He went right and we went left, so by the time we got to the turn he was barely four lengths in front. It was plain to see that Dermot Weld's stallion was making his drive for home. Aboard the mare, I hadn't even asked her for an effort. Makybe Diva simply loved this part of the race. It's here where she wants to put her head in front, where her fighting qualities simply refuse to let any other animal past. But Flemington is a long straight and I knew exactly where we wanted to hit the lead. Again, it was a game of patience. The plan was for her to be at the very peak of her sprint approaching the 200. If you have the horse capable of doing it, the issue becomes very elementary. Heading down that Flemington straight with so much raw energy still to burn, Makybe Diva was almost toying with the opposition. We knew what she was capable of when her ratings for her Cup preparation had revealed she was travelling two to three lengths better than the previous year.

She simply cruised up to them. Vinnie Roe was at the peak of his effort but when I called on the mare she swallowed the four-lengths gap and flew past to open up a one-length lead. The gutsy import chased and chased hard but, once in front, The Diva was never going to let another horse head her.

My heart was performing cartwheels of sheer delight. The previous year I had been so relieved that, whatever happened in the rest of my riding career, I would be able to retire in the knowledge that I had won a Melbourne Cup. Now, as Makybe Diva swept past the post by a length and three-quarters to the chasing field, I knew that we had become part of history. Two Melbourne Cups meant that here was a racing story to rank right up there with the greatest Cup yarns of them all. Winning once was fantastic. But this was 10 times better.

On my wall at home hangs a giant framed photo of the closing moments of the race. Taken from a point almost directly opposite and some metres back from the winning post, it shows the mare's head and forequarters in close-up as she surged flat-out for the line. You can almost count the strands of hair in her mud-caked mane. Her head, streaming forward in that wild determination to lead, and her mighty chest are coated with a layer of Flemington slurry. But what draws the observer in is her eye, that dark glowing orb alive with intelligence and passion. Look into that black jewel and you just might glimpse the secrets of courage and desire that make such an animal run like the wind.

The Diva looked like a muddied warrior. Her mighty head and forequarters were caked in it. I was soaked to the skin, the proud colours of the Santic stable bespattered with mud. But nobody seemed to care as we returned to the weigh scale and the rapturous reception of the fans who had taken Makybe Diva to heart. Once again, I gave them a quite a show from the saddle, whooping and partying along with the best of them.

Later would come a clear analysis of what her mighty effort meant in the story of Australian racing. But, for now, it was party time.

As he had done the previous year, Tony took the entire Diva team back to Port Lincoln to party with the people of Eyre Peninsula. This time Lee Freedman came too. Also among Cup first-timers was Tamara Fauser, the soon-to-be daughter-in-law of the Santic clan. Blessed with a great voice, Tamara had recorded a song called 'Makybe Diva' to the tune of 'Fever'. It became our theme song for a fabulous party in the old tuna town.

The Makybe Diva connection had already left an enduring

legacy, especially in the friendship Sloane and I enjoyed with Tony and his family. It became a special bond. We would enjoy every minute of the ride the mare provided for us and part of that journey would be the deep and abiding friendships between the Boss mob and the family of the self-made tuna man from Port Lincoln. There is so much to learn from people like the Santics. Tony worked hard, acquired plenty then lost his fortune only to back himself and build another. He turned it all around. The stories he tells about fishing and life can hold you riveted for hours. He deserves every bit of success because he has worked so hard. Tony would prove to be as fearless a punter who ever walked on to a track. Away from the bright lights he was a generous and silent donor to charities, especially in the Port Lincoln area. The Santics remember the friends who were with them in the good times and the fair-weather friends who shot through when times were tough. Our time together with the mare would cement a lifelong friendship.

18

An all-round champion

S he was the Cups champion. Winning the Sydney Cup and two Melbourne Cups in such style over the gruelling course established The Diva as Australasia's undisputed ruler of the 3200-metre distance.

By now, Lee Freedman had well and truly recognised that in Makybe Diva he had a very special animal in his stable. In becoming the first horse since Think Big in 1974–75 to win back-to-back Melbourne Cups The Diva was already part of turf lore.

David Hall's decision to hand her on to the Freedmans would prove to be one of the most fortuitous moves in the grand career of the mighty mare. Lee was all about maximising her awesome potential and The Diva had not let him down. She was bigger, stronger and faster. But the hall-of-fame trainer knew there was more. He had a plan, one that would cause hardened race followers to doubt the trainer's wisdom; a plan that would rewrite time-honoured precepts of training and preparing Group 1 gallopers.

Most owners and trainers would be happy to have a champion two-time Melbourne Cup winner in their stable. But Lee Freedman suspected Makybe Diva was much, much more than a 3200-metre horse.

Lee wanted to turn The Diva into an all-round champion – a thoroughbred with the sheer class, courage and turn of speed to win not just grinding events like the Melbourne and Sydney Cups but the race considered the true test of greatness – the weight-for-age championship of Australasia – the Cox Plate.

The Diva was sent for a thoroughly deserved spell after her Cup victory with the idea of returning in time for the autumn campaign of 2005.

Lee's first major target of the autumn was the Australian Cup at Flemington in early March. Run over 2000 metres, it has become one of the great weigh-for-age Group 1 events, a race for champions like Saintly, Octagonal, Sunline, Northerly and Lonhro. It is a tough race, almost a 2000-metre sprint test, such is the quality of the field it attracts.

It was The Diva's first trip back to Flemington since the glory of the previous November. Perhaps it was the appearance of the great mare in the field that convinced the other jockeys that they would have to set a cracking pace to try and sap some of her staying capabilities. Whatever the reason, the field fairly flew out of the barriers and kept going. They were travelling that fast the mare was almost chasing them. But at the 600, she joined in and it was as good as over. In the charge for home she just blew them away, smashing Northerly's 2000-metres record in the process. The great West Australian had set the time on a lightning fast track and many judges believed it would never be bettered. But, on a track rated as 'good' the mare had run an amazing time of 1:58:73. At that stage, we were still coming to grips with her potential. On 12 March 2005, in one blistering performance, the mare had given us yet another glimpse of her greatness.

There was no time to dwell on the success. The following Saturday she was booked for an equally important date in Sydney on Golden Slipper day at Rosehill Gardens. Autumn carnival fever had taken hold and the harbour city's race fans licked their lips in anticipation of what promised to be the showdown of the season.

Gai Waterhouse's stable star Grand Armee had been in slashing form and was expected to be at the absolute pinnacle of performance for the BMW, a Group 1 weight-for-age classic over 2400 metres. In all the history of Australian racing nobody had forged a more formidable reputation than Tommy Smith for having a horse absolutely ripe for the big carnivals and this was a trait Gai had inherited from her legendary dad. We knew that Grand Armee would definitely be right up to the mark for Rosehill.

As for the mare, she had to be floated to Sydney and then re-adjust to running in a clockwise direction within the week after an extremely tough run at Flemington. And, as opposed to Randwick where she had won the Sydney Cup, Rosehill was not necessarily The Diva's happiest hunting ground. She had never proven herself on the track. Alongside her undoubted ability they seemed small factors, but in the risk-ridden world of racing they can add up to reason enough for a punter to place his money elsewhere.

The Diva was floated up to Sydney on the Tuesday night, arriving early on Wednesday. We galloped her on the Thursday at Randwick. When I hopped off her I asked Lee: 'How confident were you about winning the Australian Cup last week?'

'I was very, very confident she wouldn't be beat,' was his answer.

'Well,' I said, 'you can be more confident this Saturday. She will win.'

In the BMW they went at a pretty solid speed. Never before had she struggled with the tempo. But this day she did. Instead of taking up a handy position just off the pace, she was getting well back. We were giving them more of a start than I would have wished. Not moving at her fluid best, she was chasing to stay in touch. At the 1200-metre mark I was thinking that she would finish well, but this would not be her race. At the 1000-metre mark she started to get going. But we were still at least 12 lengths from the lead. Was she a chance? Surely not – not from here. At the half mile, a ridiculous notion jumped into my head: 'This thing is gunna win!' We came wide around the turn and she was fairly eating up ground. With a little more than 500 metres to go she was giving Grand Armee eight lengths. With 400 to go, Gai's galloper was still six lengths in front. No horse could possibly give a polished opponent such a start and expect to run it down. But, on this day, Rosehill was about to witness something approaching a miracle.

I knew that when Makybe Diva hit peak revs there was no galloper in the Southern Hemisphere who could go with her. But logic dictated that the margin was way too great. However, there was nothing logical about the mare's courage. Like a comet closing on an unsuspecting planet, she came roaring from nowhere at high speed. By any conventional standard, Grand Armee should have won the race untouched and Makybe Diva should have finished a gallant second, beaten by two or three lengths. Nobody would have thought the less of her if that's how it had panned out. But her amazing ability to sprint at the end of a gruelling contest, plus her primitive desire to place herself at the head of the mob, delivered a finish that witnesses will remember forever. At the 200-metre mark I felt like standing up in the irons and letting rip with the biggest victory celebration of them all. 'This thing is home!' I was telling myself in a mixture of euphoria and pure disbelief. 'This thing is home!'

We went past Grand Armee in a blur and a few bounds later I was up out of the saddle giving the crowd the high fives. The winning margin was two lengths.

The capacity Rosehill crowd stood for 10 disbelieving minutes giving The Diva an uninterrupted standing ovation. Many would have known with absolute certainty that no matter how many race meetings they attended in the rest of their days, they would never see the likes of this again.

It's fair to say that her victory in the BMW that day upstaged the Golden Slipper. In a great show of respect, Paul Perry, who trained the Slipper winner Stratum, put it all in perspective when he said during the post-meeting presentations what a privilege it had been to be at Rosehill that day to witness Makybe Diva's performance.

In my humble opinion it was her finest victory.

By the spring of 2005 The Diva would have been claimed as 'the people's horse'. But, looking back, I think it was on that unforgettable Slipper day that the racing public of Australia truly took her to their hearts. Some gallopers are forever associated with wherever they are trained or bred. After all, racing is a parochial game, especially at carnival time when the best gallopers travel from interstate on missions to beat Sydney's or Melbourne's best in their own backyards. So it takes something really special for the average fan to abandon his or her local loyalty and embrace a galloper irrespective of where it might call home. Tony Santic's syndicate was The Diva's official owner, but now they would have to share her with the rest of Australia. Just about everybody it seemed had an emotional stake in the fortunes of the grand mare.

When people talk about their favourite horses they often mention a brilliant colt or gelding. But give me a good tough mare any day. They won't be denied. They just keep stepping up and demanding more. For whatever reason they are more durable and seem to have a higher pain threshold. The harder it gets the more they dig in. Such was The Diva. Yet, as tough and hard as she was she still had a certain elegance – a sexiness almost. Charisma. She was marvellously proportioned, her markings were in all the right places and the classic thorough-bred shape of her head gave her a noble bearing.

After her brilliant autumn in Sydney, the pressure was on for the mare to prove her worth in Japan on the international stage. The Japanese campaign was to cruelly reveal the one chink in her armour: her intolerance to flint-hard surfaces.

She ran seventh at Nakayama on 10 April and despite being in obvious discomfort every time she put a hoof on the rock-like ground, she still tried to race. The major assignment was the Tenno Sho (Emperor's Cup) on 1 May, a rich weight-for-age event over 3200 metres. It being her preferred distance, the mare was sent out as favourite. But, despite rain on the day of the race, the Kyoto track was like concrete. She struggled all the way, doing her best despite the pain, and finished seventh.

Footsore and travel weary, Makybe Diva returned to Australia and a welcome rest.

The approach of spring brought with it another stroke of genius from Lee Freedman. Like most stayers, Makybe Diva would work her way into a campaign, taking time to reach that rare pitch of fitness and aggression that enabled her to dominate her opponents. But Lee had an idea – he wanted her to win first up back from a spell. He knew she could stay and he also knew she had a great turn of foot. According to Lee's plan, she would return in the spring as a sprinter and then step up in distance until she was ready to take on the cream of the crop in the Cox Plate.

I rarely rode her first up and, anyway, I was suspended at the time and couldn't have claimed the ride. My recommendation was that Steven King would be ideal for the job. My reasoning was that not only was he a brilliant rider, he had wonderful hands, great timing, a relaxed demeanour and really knew how to look after a horse. With Kingy, I knew she would be in safe care.

We spoke on the phone. 'Don't ever think you're in a position where you can't win,' I told him, 'because she will do freakish things. She's that good.'

Steven took on the best sprinters in Australia in the Group 2 Memsie Stakes over 1400 metres at Caulfield, gave them a good start and just towelled them up.

Steven had ridden some of the best, including the brilliant Let's Elope, but after the Memsie he said with a touch of awe in his voice, 'I've never ridden anything like it!'

Next start, I was back on the mare for the Group 2 Feehan Stakes over the 1600-metre distance at Moonee Valley. A Japanese import set an unsustainable pace out front and we were left tailing the field. Lad Of The Manor won the race but, again, Makybe Diva came flashing home late to grab a close second. Considering how far back she had been, the mare had no right whatsoever to get that close.

With my attention taken up by Group 1 commitments in Sydney, Kingy was back on her for the 2000 metres, Turnbull Stakes at Flemington, the mare's last run before the Cox Plate. In a field of 16, there were only three horses behind the mare 800 metres from home. Steven rode her to perfection and she swooped on the field to win by three-quarters of a length. Our prime target, the Cox Plate, was just 21 days away and Makybe Diva was still to reach peak fitness. The Freedman plan was running like clockwork.

19

A mad sprint to victory

Boxers go into camp to prepare for a title fight. In October, I packed my bags and flew to Melbourne for the spring campaign. For me, this is the most serious and intense phase of the racing calendar, a time for total focus on the job at hand. Of course, there would be other horses to ride in Melbourne in the spring of 2005, but my main mission was to put the finishing touches to one of the boldest plans in Australian racing: guiding Makybe Diva to victory in the Cox Plate.

The thoroughbred that greeted me on my return to track work was bigger and stronger than ever. Amazingly, at seven years of age, she was still packing on the muscle and her coat was again dappling up as she approached peak fitness. It was a formidable sight and I could sense my excitement rising at the prospect of being aboard this giant of a mare for the looming battle in the amphitheatre that is Moonee Valley racecourse.

Lee proposed a mini rehearsal by booking her in for a searching gallop at the Valley a full week before the big race. With Steven King on the accompanying galloper, a renowned plugger, the idea was to go at three-quarter speed for 2000 metres to the 600-metre mark where Steven was meant to shake up his mount to give the mare something to chase. He shook it up all right. At the 600-metre mark, he simply took off and put six lengths on us in a blink. The acceleration certainly surprised Kingy and left me wondering what I was supposed to do – take off in pursuit at the risk of pushing The Diva or give it away as a bad idea? Lee must have been tearing his hair out. The mare had her own ideas. I gave her just one dig in the ribs and *bang* she just went for the horse in front, up the hill, around the bend and blazed past him in the straight to win clear by about five lengths. The clockers were opened-mouth in sheer amazement. At first I thought I had stuffed up because she blew more after that effort than she had done after most of her races. But, once again, after a minute or so her breathing was right back to normal.

Lee had never wanted her to go anywhere near that fast a week before the big race and the look on his face suggested we might have overcooked her at a vital time. But, by then she was her old, relaxed self, chewing away at the grass. Never had I encountered a galloper with such a recovery rate.

'Don't worry about it,' I said with a grin. 'That's just how she is.'

You can't afford to make a mistake at Moonee Valley. Compared with Flemington's wide open spaces, it is a tight arena with a short, unforgiving straight. One bad check or error of judgement and there is no way back. It's a saucer-like track and the way the spectator areas pack the fans close to the action makes for a unique and exciting racing atmosphere.

When the pundits went looking for a chink in Makybe Diva's armour they noted that she was still a maiden at the Valley. Sure, she had gone close once or twice but, unlike just about everywhere else, she was yet to win there.

Lee had her perfectly conditioned and primed, ready to go. In her own way, The Diva always reminded us when she was right at the top of her game. Yes, there was that extra dapple in the coat but, more importantly, she would become more aggressive, less ladylike and more like a warrior sensing the heat of the battle ahead. That's how she was in the final countdown to the Cox Plate, the culmination of a daring strategy to establish her as the all-round galloping champion of Australasia.

However, the enormity of the task that would face us in the Cox Plate had become evident after I had ridden one of The Diva's main competitors on Saturday 8 October.

On that day I was down to ride the lightly raced colt God's Own in the $1 million Group 1 Caulfield Guineas over 1600 metres. The Cox Plate may be the real headline grabber of the Melbourne carnival but the Guineas stands as a super race in its own right. Who could forget Our Maizcay's bold effort in 1995 when he defied the likes of Octagonal? Or the following year when Alfa, Intergaze and Encosta De Lago staged a ding-dong battle? In 1999 it was virtually a match race as Redoute's Choice and Testa Rossa slugged it out down the length of the straight. Two years later, the mighty Lonhro emerged from the Guineas as the best three-year-old in the land.

The Guineas class of 2005 lived right up to and, possibly exceeded, those awesome standards. It was a who's who of the star two-year-olds from the previous year with Paul Perry's Golden Slipper winner Stratum, the brilliant Paratroopers, Perfectly Ready, Red Dazzler, Apache Cat, Gonski and Primus all featuring in the betting. Among them was God's Own, a handsome son of Redoute's Choice who, since starting his stud career in 2000, had taken the breeding world by storm.

Carrying the colours of black and white checks with yellow sleeves made famous by former champion Saintly, God's Own looked an absolute picture in the mounting yard. Like Saintly, he was trained by Bart Cummings and had been picked up at the Inglis Classic Sales for what would prove to be a bargain $220,000.

When the gates opened, Darren Beadman had Paratroopers out quick and slick to settle behind early leader Gonski. My colt was well tucked away in midfield looking to make ground as the field approached the 1000-metre mark.

When a horse in front cops a bad check, the chain reaction ripples right through the following runners. That's what happened when Paternity suffered interference going up the hill and dropped back suddenly into Primus, who then cannoned into God's Own firing the colt out the back into last position. He was shaken up but I steadied him and got his mind back on the job to make some ground in the run to the turn. Everybody else had kept going wide so we cut the corners on the inside. Despite the earlier check, we were just behind the leaders in what looked to me like a winning position and we still had a little gas in the tank. Another split appeared in front of us and, just as we made our move, a runner came from the inside, straight under my colt's neck. He almost fell and we were sent clattering into

Red Dazzler. I was all but out of the saddle as Paratroopers took off for home. It was a miracle that God's Own managed to stay on his feet but what happened in the next 30 seconds or so simply defied belief. With me swearing at the offending jockey as we shot past, God's Own set off in pursuit of the leaders. So far the Guineas had been more like a prize fight than a Group 1 race, but my colt was still in there punching.

With Gonski and Paratroopers still leading, it looked like God's Own was going to run a miraculous, if unlucky, third. But the colt had other ideas. Head down, his ears flat, with each huge stride he went at the Caulfield straight like a starving man at a rump steak. With half a furlong to go, Paratroopers appeared to have too much of a lead but God's Own descended like a thunderbolt from heaven. We grabbed Paratroopers 20 metres from the line and with a couple of ground-swallowing strides swept into the lead for the first time. The winning margin was by a long neck, with Primus making a late surge to nudge Gonski out of third place.

It was an incredible victory and definitely one of the most unforgettable of my career. The three-year-old colt having only his fifth start had performed like a seasoned champion to survive two near knockdowns, pick himself up and chase one of the hottest fields you would find anywhere. Catching the leaders was a feat in itself. Passing them all to win his first Group 1, well, that was just unbelievable. Even Bart Cummings, with hundreds of Group 1 wins to his name, was shocked.

God's Own had shouted a declaration to the racing world and was on his way to the Cox Plate, where he would carry a mere 48 kilograms. In winning the Guineas in such style, he had put us all on notice. Makybe Diva would have to run the race of her life to prevent God's Own becoming the first horse since the mighty Red Anchor in 1984 to collect the Caulfield Guineas – Cox Plate double.

I hardly slept on the Friday night before the Plate. That was unusual for me. My nerves were jangling and I knew why.

Partly to allay my own nerves I laid out my race plans to the owner and the trainer.

'I will not ride her pretty,' I said. 'I'm gunna sit one off the fence and I don't care if I have to go round the outside fence. It won't be pretty. In fact, it might be ugly. But I'll get the job done.'

And that's how it worked out.

In my journey from boyhood to mature jockey the Cox Plate and Moonee Valley held a special place in my dreams. Those old highlights reels of Manikato – The Man – at his untouchable best featured the Valley packed to the rafters to cheer on the champ. And it was here at Moonee Valley where Malcolm Johnston and Kingston Town got so far back in the Cox Plate that the doyen of race callers, Bill Collins, declared The King couldn't win and then watched in amazement as one of the greatest gallopers ever to step onto a track simply mowed them down. And now, so many years later, here was I on a thoroughbred with the potential to take her place alongside the legends of the turf, carrying the weight of history and expectation in my none-too-steady hands. As the 14 race jockeys were presented one at a time before the running of the Plate, I reminded myself what were here for: 'Relax, stay focused, remember your race plan.'

Tony Santic played his own part in ensuring the 2005 Cox

Plate day was a fun event. It was his wish that the mare become the people's horse and to that end he invited the 'Diva Believers' to get in on the party and distributed thousands of masks in the red, white and blue of his racing silks.

Despite the proximity and din of the capacity crowd, Makybe Diva was her usual relaxed self on the way to the barrier. This was the race she had been set for and she was in magnificent shape – coat gleaming and her attitude all bullish-aggression as she felt the rising tide of her strength and fitness. She was primed to the absolute minute.

Barrier draws were never really an issue with her as she invariably jumped well and settled into her customary position about two-thirds of the way back in the field. But, on settling down and with the pace just so-so, I noted we were fractionally farther back than I would have wanted for the 2040-metre journey. Yet, I wasn't really worried because by about the halfway mark she was getting on the bridle and starting to feel pretty good. At the 1000-metre mark I moved out to improve position when Xcellent, an athletic four-year-old stayer, took off. 'Here we go,' I thought, 'they're trying to flush us out.'

God's Own, the brilliant three-year-old colt and Guineas winner ridden by Steve Baster, joined in the chase and in a twinkling it seemed that more than half of the field were in a charge for home. 'Do I sit back and let them go and then try to chase them down?' I wondered. In a split second I had my answer: we had to go with them. 'This wasn't in the script,' I said to myself as I pulled The Diva out, looking for room to improve. With the shake of her tail she went from rolling along to sprint speed. At the 700 we were five-wide in a crush of horses, all full of running, none backing off as the best chances muscled up for the run home. They had all got impatient and were trying to flush her out. Suddenly, it had turned into a staying contest. The Diva was absolutely hungry to go with them, her appetite for the fight white hot. But I didn't want her getting there too soon and had to pull her back under me.

It's in these intense racing moments that you glimpse the primitive instincts of the herd. The prodigious colts like God's Own, sensing their masculinity and flatly determined to dominate their rivals – especially a mare – would rather die trying than give a centimetre to another thoroughbred. Almost every runner in the field had joined in a mad sprint for the line.

So, in this way, the spectators at the turn were treated to one of the most blood-stirring sights in Australian racing. Like the charge of the Light Brigade, we banked through that final turn 11 abreast, iron-to-iron, as the Group 1 blue bloods attempted to out-muscle and out-sprint each other for the championship of Australasia. Later, the action replays would show the front-on shot of the field. It was a truly awe-inspiring sight. A wall of horses shoulder to shoulder across the track. No room for faint hearts here. The slightest flicker of doubt by horse or rider could consign you to the also-runs.

As the field fanned out I had moved The Diva wider and wider looking for a gap. We were a full nine wide as I poked her into a space just inside Xcellent and God's Own. 'Whoa, whoa!' I called to her, again pulling The Diva in. Immediately inside me was Steven King on the 2003 Cox Plate winner Fields Of Omagh who also looked full of running. Kingy shot me a glance as if to say: 'What about this!' It was like an over-crowded dance floor as the wall of horseflesh bumped, barged and jostled for clean air.

By now some of the horses that had gone early were dying on their runs. But I was wary of those gallopers who hadn't spent a penny and were now looking for the short way home on the inside. One of them was Gai Waterhouse's Lotteria, bound to arrive for a late crack at the leaders.

As I predicted, it wasn't pretty but The Diva and I were where we wanted to be. At the top of the straight she hit the front for the first time in the race and nothing was going to stop her. The hard work and sweat had been done. From that point it was elementary, hands-and heels all the way to the line. Fields Of Omagh and Lotteria staged a ding-dong fight for second with Kingy's mount prevailing by a half head. But neither could get near Makybe Diva as she raced into history by a clear one-and-quarter lengths.

In all of sport there is nothing better than watching a wonderful athlete at the very top of their game displaying their greatness for all to see. That was Makybe Diva on Cox Plate day 2005.

Races of 3200 metres can be gut-busters for the average horse. But Makybe Diva had shown she could eat up that sort of distance and ask for more. However, this challenge had been different. To win she had to sprint with them a long way from home and then go ultra-wide looking for a good position to run. The horses that had gone with her early had finished 15 lengths away. She had run them off their legs. But the effort had taken its toll. Every sinew in her body had been tested. Everything she had to give had been left out there on the track. For the first time after a race I was genuinely concerned about her. When we pulled up she was blowing like she had never blown before. She was almost wobbly legged. We took a long time to return to the enclosure. But by the time we had completed the in-the-saddle interview on the way back, she was almost back to her old self. It was as if she was giving me permission to get up in the irons and lair-ise in my usual way with the crowd.

On dismounting Lee asked, 'How is she?'

'She's gone!' I answered. 'She's left everything on the track.'

The master trainer didn't waste a second or assign the task to anyone else. As I headed for the weigh-in he took the mare and led her around the enclosure, keeping her moving to stop the lactic acid building up in those mighty muscles. The minutes after a demanding run can be very crucial for a horse. If pushed to a certain level of stress they can 'tie up' – a condition where the muscles in the hindquarters seize up – and are never the same again. And this Group 1 had been like a heavyweight title fight that went the full distance and then some. She had beaten Lotteria, an exceptional mare a year younger than Makybe Diva, who had taken the short way home. And she had beaten an absolute warrior in Fields Of Omagh, a brilliant colt in God's Own and the outstanding Lad Of The Manor, as well as nine of the best gallopers in the land.

She had won the greatest title fight of her life. But at what price?

20

Diva Fever

As he walked the mare in circles and figure eights after the Cox Plate, Lee Freedman was thinking. At the edge of the enclosure the racing media, notebooks and recorders at the ready, waited. He knew what they were going to ask him and he had just thought of the perfect answer.

'Are you going to run her in the Cup, Lee?'

'We'll let her decide,' he told them.

And so began one of the greatest off-the-track dramas of Australian turf history. The Melbourne Cup was still 10 days away but it seemed like there was no other story in town as the media mounted a 24-hour vigil on whether or not the mare would take a shot at an unprecedented third Cup victory.

This level of attention was beyond the normal glamour and glitz of carnival racing – it was movie star stuff complete with media stake-outs, paparazzi and constant bulletins to a nation high on Diva Fever.

By then Tony Santic knew his horse belonged to the Australian racing public, but he summed up the situation quite simply: 'The Cox Plate was her Melbourne Cup this year. That's what she was set for and she achieved that goal. She has already won two Melbourne Cups and now she doesn't have to do anything else. If she never races again she has already achieved everything we have asked of her.'

After the rigours of her Cox Plate campaign the mare must have relished her return to the peace and quiet of the Markdel property near Rye, where the sea breezes and wide open spaces allowed her to relax.

Away from Markdel and around morning coffee urns, in pub conversations, turf editorials and, particularly, within the walls of the Cup host, the Victorian Racing Club, there was a desperate desire to see Makybe Diva have a shot at history. It was a racing promoter's dream!

Some elements of the media surmised that the stable was playing a game with the public – that the decision had already been made to run her and the Freedmans and Tony Santic were just drawing out the drama. Nothing could have been further from the truth. Down at Rye, the staff kept a watching brief on the mare's progress. After four, carefree days in the paddock where she relaxed and ate well, Lee phoned on the Wednesday evening with the message to be at Rye on the Thursday to ride her in work. 'You'd better get down here, Bossy,' Lee said, with a sense of genuine amazement in his voice, 'this thing has put on 6 kilos!' Rather than being flattened by her amazing effort in the Cox Plate, the wonder horse was thriving!

On the way to Markdel it became evident just how much the 'Diva watch' had turned into a media circus. Camera crews and photographers were camping out in the scrub. Others had requisitioned carts from the nearby golf course to drive them and their gear down to the perimeter of Markdel where they could set up their big lenses in the hope of catching vision of the mare.

Lee's instructions were absolute: he didn't want me to sugar-coat the mare's performance just to guarantee myself a ride in the Melbourne Cup. He wanted the exact picture and the only being who could give us that was Makybe Diva. It would be her decision. The mare would tell us.

'It's not your call, Bossy,' Lee had said, 'it's hers.'

I worked her twice that morning and on both occasions she was breathing well when she pulled up. From my position in the saddle she felt bouncy, aggressive and eager. She felt great! The sensation of galloping her on the sand track that day is a feeling I will take with me forever. She gave me goose bumps. What a magnificent animal. I was in awe of her.

Here I had been thinking, 'We shouldn't be doing this to her.' But the clear message she was sending back was: 'I am ready to go!'

I walked her back to Lee and said, 'It is scary how good this horse is!'

And that's all he needed to know.

Yet the decision whether to run in the Cup was delayed. Remember, we had set her for the Cox Plate, not the Melbourne Cup. Lee wanted to gallop her again on the Saturday so that he was 100 per cent sure in his own mind that everything was okay. The plan was to take her out on the course at Mornington early on the Saturday morning for a very search-ing gallop. If she didn't pass that exam with top marks she wasn't running on the Tuesday.

Tony Santic and I left Markdel on the Thursday in the same

car with Lee's riding instructions ringing in our ears: 'Be poker-faced on the way out,' he had said. 'Give nothing away.'

The media posse was waiting for us at the gate with a veritable thicket of microphones and camera lens. I'd like to think that Tony and I are reasonable card players because neither of us let on that we were holding the best hand in the land five days out from the Cup.

When we finally moved on, I rang Lee on my mobile and asked, 'Can we smile now?'

The Diva continued to thrive and on the Saturday morning we took her down to Mornington for the gallop that would determine her Cup fate. As with the previous year, we sent her out in the company of another horse but this time I was a trifle concerned. Southern Australia had been in the grip of a protracted drought and the track at Mornington was a bit too firm for her liking. And if it wasn't right for her, it wasn't right for any of us. But there was no turning back. We had to do the work. If she pulled up sore, we wouldn't be running her on the Tuesday.

We sent the other horse out over the 2000 metres with The Diva in pursuit. She felt a little bit jarry when she put her feet down but it wasn't too bad. Again, she gave the other horse plenty of start and beat it well with smart sectional times on the firm track. I took forever to pull her up for the simple reason that I wanted plenty of time to go through the entire check list to find out how she had handled the gallop. I knew that if she wanted to pull up quick it meant that we had hurt her, so I kept her going at a slowing gallop. She was fine.

When I brought her back, Lee asked the simple question: 'What do you think?'

I simply nodded.

Enough said.

The media crush at Mornington that day was so big it could have passed for a race day crowd. As Lee unsaddled the mare, the press pack converged on him. Momentarily left on our own, the Santics and I ducked out the side and jumped into the car to make our getaway. Before I could reverse out, the media were on us:

'What's the decision? What's the decision?' they hounded us.

'Look, Lee will let us know when he gets her back to the property, has a close look at exactly how she's pulled up and sees if she sticks her head in the feed bin.'

The media, knowing that acceptances would be declared that day, were frantic.

'Lee will let you know,' I said as we pulled away.

But after that gallop I already knew the answer. She was perfect. As soon as we were on our own, I turned to Tony with a grin and said: 'It's on again, mate. It's on again. She'll win.'

Monday evening found me out at Flemington for a television interview. With a bit of time to kill I took a stroll on the track. I must have walked half a circuit and every step confirmed what I needed to know. There was enough moisture underfoot. Come Tuesday morning, I knew it would be a perfect racing surface. The last piece of the puzzle had clicked into place.

We stuck to the game plan. On the Monday night Tony and

I had a couple of beers at the Crown Hotel and talked about destiny.

'It's like you're on a runaway train and it can't be stopped,' I said. 'The wheels have been set in motion and there's nothing going to stand in its way. She will win. You can't come this far and not win.'

As a jockey, I've never been one for the early crow – never – but it felt like the right thing to say at the time.

With a couple of 'see ya tomorrows' Tony and I bid each other good night and I went back to my digs and slept like a lamb. The next morning I was up early feeling refreshed and relaxed. In the media, another drama concerning Makybe Diva was playing out. Nobody in her camp wanted the mare to run on a flint hard track. However, despite the drought, the Flemington authorities had assured us the track would have enough give in it. They even went so far to make sure the track was well-watered. The last impediment had been removed.

From the moment I passed through the gates at Flemington I was convinced Tuesday 1 November 2005 was going to be one of my greatest days of racing. For starters, it was a radiant spring day and it was pure fun just to be there. Secondly, the omens were right. Amid all the media calls I was happy to take that morning came the customary call from a couple of mates on a Gold Coast radio station. As we chatted I looked up to note that I was underneath the same advertising board at the same time and place as the previous two Melbourne Cups when they had called. 'History was repeating,' I told myself.

Everywhere you looked at Flemington, fans were wearing The Diva masks.

No sporting event on the calendar is subject to as much speculation as the Cup. The early betting markets on the day had the John Hawkes–trained Railings, winner of the Caulfield Cup, shading The Diva for favouritism. Astute judges rate the Caulfield Cup as one of the most accurate pointers to the eventual Melbourne Cup winner and for that reason there was plenty of money for the 'Corowa Comet' Leica Falcon, a fast-finishing fifth behind Railings. And then there was the multiple Irish St Leger winner Vinnie Roe. It would be the veteran import's last start and his wily trainer Dermot Weld wanted nothing more than the stallion to annexe Australia's richest race before heading off to stud.

Makybe Diva was aiming to become the first horse to win the Australian Cup, the BMW and the Cox Plate in a calendar year. The back half of that effort had taken a tremendous toll on the seven-year-old. Would she have enough left in the tank to win an endurance handicap like the Cup? And, the pundits pointed out, she was attempting to defy history. Not since 1904, when Acrasia took the trophy, had a seven-year-old mare won the race. No mare had lugged 58 kilograms around Flemington to win the Cup. In fact, not since 1975 when Think Big carted 58.5 kilograms to victory had a winner been saddled with a similar weight. I had done plenty of homework on Cup weight and spoken to a number of knowledgeable people. Jim Bowler, the man who had served as handicapper on many Melbourne Cups, had said he would have handi-capped her like a colt or gelding. He thought she was that superior. I had come to the conclusion that weight wasn't an issue for the mare.

There were a hundred arguments and omens as to why she couldn't win the big race. But none of them stacked up alongside the most compelling truth of them all: she was a champion. I knew she would win. As for her, it was business as usual. In her race-day stall, amid the din and hubbub of Cup day at Flemington, she had quietly dozed off.

Champions simply refuse to be beaten. I can remember a trainer telling me about a classy horse that he had set for a Group 1 race only to scratch it when it was stung by a bee. It made me think about how champions seems to shake off any setbacks and get on with the job. People would say we had our share of luck with Makybe Diva. But I tend to think her desire to race meant she overcame the sort of things that would have stopped other horses.

Perhaps the racing public sensed that too. Or maybe they were all just a bunch of romantics who wanted to see the queen of the turf's fairytale come true. Whatever the reason, the great punting public of Australia backed her in to start a $4.40 favourite for the 144th running of the great race.

21

Nothing left to prove

Makybe Diva carried the number 1 saddlecloth and for the second time in three years she had drawn barrier 14. Lee and I had discussed race tactics the previous evening. With her weight I didn't want her anchored in the early stages so I was planning to be a bit more aggressive from the start than in the previous two years. Lee's thinking was to play the percentages, have us out and in the clear, but my strategy was to get her as close to the fence as possible. I didn't think I could come around the field with her carrying such a big weight. My thinking was to ride her as I had done before. It had worked every time. Why change a good thing? Lee thought about that and said: 'Well, you are a lucky bastard. Just go out there and do your thing.'

Lee Freedman had put me on horses when I was a junior jockey riding in Brisbane. When I arrived in Sydney he was already a superstar among trainers, having became the first trainer to win the Caulfield Cup, Melbourne Cup, Cox Plate and Golden Slipper in one season. I'll be forever indebted to Lee for giving me the chance on Flying Spur for my first major Group 1 success in the Golden Slipper. As I've related earlier, there were any number of reasons why I shouldn't have been on the horse and why he shouldn't have won. But, together, we got the job done against the odds and I don't think Lee forgot that. In some ways he had launched my Group 1 career but never in my wildest dreams would I have imagined the Freedman-Boss connection would have found its way to such a long and sustaining partnership as the one we enjoyed with Makybe Diva. Riding for the Freedman brothers would turn out to be one of the most enjoyable facets of the game. They were great people to be around and Lee's knowledge was peerless. When he spoke, it paid to listen. He never had much to say, but when he did, it was usually gold. We had built a great bond during the time with the mare. I trusted his judgement completely and he reciprocated.

On race days he only ever had two lines of wisdom for me: 'Sharp mind. Cool head'. He repeated his mantra there in the enclosure. I had rarely felt so calm or clear-headed in my life. I was in 'The Zone'.

On the way to the barrier The Diva felt absolutely brilliant. Believe it or not, she had come on again since the Cox Plate. Like a warhorse thriving on the smell of battle, the aggression was coursing through her. The sensation that flowed up to me through the saddle was one of a mighty racing machine girding itself for another great contest. The Cox Plate should have drained her but in the space of 10 days she had come back bigger, better than ever. My awe and admiration climbed another few notches.

We jumped cleanly and I gave her a real dig to drive her up in search of a spot on the inside. We may have got a bit farther back than I would have desired but within a furlong we had found the fence. The tempo was pretty genuine. Then, whoa! A horse at the front copped a bad check and came back on us. The Diva didn't panic. She simply stopped on a dime and then resumed her journey. 'How good is this,' I thought. We were in a great position and she relaxed straightaway into that beautiful rhythmic stride. Beneath me she felt like a grand machine in 'sleep' mode. It was déjà vu. The race was unfolding as it had in the previous years. At the 1600 I was chuckling: 'It can't be like this. It can't be this easy.' I've been beaten on horses when I was totally convinced we were going to win. But this was different. Everything about The Diva felt right. That's how well she was travelling. And, as the gaps appeared in front of us, we simply eased our way forward.

It was uncanny. I was so completely in 'The Zone' that everything seemed to happen automatically. I could see so clearly that I was pre-empting every move 100 metres ahead. In some ways, it was panning out easier than the previous two Cups.

Then, the pace came on. When the runs started to come, the mare's competitive spirit fired up and she wanted to go. However, there was no need as she was already trucking up through them without using too much gas. Once again I held her up, knowing almost to the very blade of grass where I wanted her to be flat out at the peak of her sprint. With about half a dozen horses in front of us, she was right where she needed to be. I hadn't wanted to go too early, nor did I need to leave it too late. With the weight she was carrying, if I asked her to sprint too late the others just might get the drop on us. As she bound past the 300-metre mark I said: 'Let's go!' and she pinned back her ears and went for home like a runaway express train with its furnace fully stoked.

When she surged forward the roar of the crowd hit us like a mighty wave. Here was history unfolding before their eyes. We were a full 200 metres from home when she grabbed the lead. Flemington was virtually erupting. It was all over. Nothing was going to catch us. In that final furlong I could hear the crowd roaring louder than a jet engine. On A Jeune arrived fast and late but, between the mare and her rider, we had judged it to perfection with a length and a quarter to spare as we hit the line. I'm certain I will win another Cup and it will be special in its own way. But nothing will ever replicate the feeling I experienced up there on the mighty mare as she galloped to immortality.

And that's how it played out. Lee Freedman would say later that they should take each of my winning Cup rides and bottle them for posterity as exercises in perfection. But so commanding was The Diva on this day that I felt like I could have taken my hands off the reins and let her do it all by herself. When she hit the front it felt like 106,000 people lifted as one to watch a great thoroughbred enter the realm of legends.

We took a long time to return to the mounting yard. Again, The Diva was blowing hard, but not as hard as her opponents. However, this time she had spent every penny. Whereas she had walked out on to Flemington with head high, now it drooped in near exhaustion. There was nothing left. I stopped her in the middle of the track and let the thunderous applause wash over us. In a mark of respect for what she had achieved, the other riders let her return to the yard on her own.

As the clerk of the course led us down the race to the enclosure, I threw victory signs of pure jubilation. Cameras snapped and the crowd rose to acclaim a new legend of the turf.

And, yes, I shed more than a few tears. At the realisation that everything – yes, everything – had worked out exactly as it should and that this would almost certainly be my final outing with the mare, my emotions burst like a dam. So much for the sharp mind, cool head.

Awaiting her approach, Lee sensed the mare had run her last race. He said later that he could read Tony Santic's thoughts and knew the proud owner was thinking the same thing. My words confirmed what the trainer's expert eye had already detected: 'She had nothing left to give,' I told him. The statistics bore me out: her winning time of 3:19:17 was the fastest of her three Cup wins.

On dismounting, I jumped straight into the arms of Tony Santic. It was a giant hug – part pure joy and part empathy for the decision I knew he was about to make.

At the presentation ceremony Lee stepped up to the microphone and uttered the words that ushered the most worthy of mares into a richly deserved retirement: 'It has been a great ride but I think it has come to an end in a perfect way.'

Makybe Diva had galloped into retirement and immortality.

The record would show that she started 36 times for 15 wins, four seconds and three thirds for total prize money of $14,526,685 – an Australasian record.

Before she had returned to the enclosure on that unforgettable Tuesday the comparisons with Phar Lap, the greatest legend of the Australian turf, were already underway.

'I don't want to put Phar Lap down,' said Lee Freedman, 'but I never saw him win three Melbourne Cups.'

The trainer also compared her effort with Cathy Freeman's run in the final of the 400-metres at the Sydney Olympics and Keiren Perkins' against-the-odds victory in the 1500-metres final in Atlanta.

Then he put it all into context: 'Go out and find the smallest child here because that child might be the only person who lives long enough to see something like this again.'

Somewhere amid the tears and joy of the post-race crush I managed to find Sloane. We simply fell into each others arms and hung on tight. My life partner who had accompanied me every step of the way, who had not queried my impulsive decision to move south all those years ago, who held my hand through those dark hours in Macau, knew exactly what this moment meant.

SLOANE: 'This one was the best of them all. I can never remember Glen being so relaxed the night before a big race. He said, "I've ridden this horse so many times but she just keeps getting better and better." He believed they would win. Meanwhile, I kept thinking: "What about the other horses?" But Glen was confident. Some of our friends and family from the Gold Coast and Sydney hadn't been able to make it to Melbourne for the previous two, so they all turned up this time. It was an unbelievable day. Knowing Glen as well as I do, I was in the position to understand just how much it meant to him. It will be a long time before I am able to think about that day without getting goose bumps.'

Knowing that you have helped etch a small part in Australian racing history is a wonderful feeling. Being associated with such a magnificent athlete like the mare is truly humbling. I particularly appreciated the trust created firstly with David Hall and then later with Lee Freedman. It helped build a collaborative environment in which we were able to work out what best suited the mare. All the players in the drama came together like a collection of gears that somehow meshed perfectly to allow the thoroughbred to be her best.

Not everybody was gracious about Makybe Diva's victory. A few connections wanted to tarnish her triumph by whinging about the Victorian Racing Club's decision to water the track a day or so before the Cup. Tony and Lee had made it quite clear that the mare would not be running on a flint hard track. Some horses like the rock-hard going but the truth of the matter is it does more horses harm than good. If thoroughbreds were meant to run on such surfaces we'd be holding meetings on disused airport tarmacs rather than well-turfed racecourses. The irony was that the few who were doing the complaining were associated with horses that finished well back in the field. Their gallopers had been beaten by 20 or 30 lengths. As I told one media outlet: 'She would have run down a bitumen road to beat any of those horses.'

As great a racehorse as she had been, Makybe Diva left me with the impression that she will prove to be a great breeding mare. She always had a certain pizazz about her that went well with her wonderful demeanour. She would never kick or bite – she was too much of a lady. On the field she was powerful and aggressive, but away from the action she had a wonderful feminine side to her. I'm betting those genes will show through as her offspring step out into the world.

22

Lady Luck goes missing

As we counted down the shopping days to Christmas 2005, the racing game was still abuzz with word of the mare responsible for one of the most outstanding feats in the long and spectacular history of the turf.

In an era when the Melbourne Cup had evolved from a Southern Hemisphere race to an international classic, Makybe Diva had stunned the world by winning over the gruelling distance for a third time. In many ways, she had received what she so richly deserved – recognition for her greatness – but, above all, a welcome ticket to the retirement paddock. Meanwhile, there would be little rest for anyone associated with her exploits.

As the jockey lucky enough to have been on her back throughout the three Cup campaigns, my world was turned on its head. From all points of the sporting and corporate compass came invitations and offers to endorse products, make public appearances, deliver after-dinner speeches and add my name to a particular promotion. Of course, everybody making those offers would have preferred to see the mare in the flesh. Instead, they had to settle for the next best – the bloke who rode her. In the space of three minutes or so on a Tuesday afternoon of November 2005, I had graduated from being a notable entity in the world of jockeys to the A-list of Australian sporting celebrities. Now, I don't say that as a bragging point but more as an indication of just how hectic life was to become in the wake of that third Cup win.

Nothing stalls a rider's career more quickly than taking too long to enjoy the view. Racing is all about 'next' – the next race, next meeting, next carnival, next talented horse to ride. Spend too long looking in the rear-view mirror and the world passes you by. So, once the celebrations were all done and dusted, my plan was to jump straight back on to the broad back of my career and reinforce my reputation as 'Group 1 Glen', the jockey with the appetite for the big ones.

One horse with the potential to help me do just that was Eremein.

He had come to my attention as a two-year-old when I had the good fortune to win on him. Trained by Allan Denham, the colt was another from the long list of outstanding horses bred and raced by Geoff and Beryl White of the Invermein Stud near Scone in the Hunter Valley. The Whites had long been great supporters of mine. Back then, Eremein was a skinny little thing, but he had a tonne of talent.

We might have been reunited during his early three-year-old days but, instead, I was on the Bob Thomsen–trained Jymcarew to win the Gosford Guineas and then the Canterbury Guineas (with Eremein second), heading towards the Rosehill Guineas and the Australian Derby at Randwick. As it turned out, the part-nership of jockey Corey Brown and Eremein were too good for us in both races.

My guess was that Eremein would spell for the winter and return for the spring of 2005. Instead, he raced in Brisbane where he broke down after chipping both knees when Activation beat him by a nose in the Rough Habit Plate at Doomben. Eremein would have been a red-hot favourite for the Queensland Derby but his knees forced the Denhams to pull the plug on the campaign, and the galloper headed for a date with the surgeon. It would be autumn 2006 before he finally made it back to big-time racing. Corey was engaged in Hong Kong so I asked Allan if I could ride Eremein. It was a bit of a punt on my part because most horses do not return too well after suffering knee problems. Also against him was the fact that he was a son of Timber Country who, despite a smart racing career in the US, had yet to prove himself as a sire in Australia. Yet his dam Marrego was a good'un and I had liked the feel of Eremein as a two-year-old. In my quest to find the next Group 1 champ after The Diva's exit, my estimation was that the Whites' galloper just might be the forgotten horse with a few surprises left in his arsenal. Also, the bone chips removed from his knees weren't big and, with his status as a gelding ruling out his stud prospects, the obvious option was to per-severe with his racing career. The stable was confident he was over the worst of his knee problems. Uppermost in my thinking was that but for the fact that my mount had beaten him by a neck in the Canterbury Guineas, Eremein would have won the three-year-old Triple Crown. In other words, he had the potential to be a superstar.

I rode him in an 800-metre barrier trial at Rosehill in

January 2006. He was fat, hairy and way below true fitness but he felt absolutely right. I could hardly contain my excitement. Despite his less-than-flash appearance and the fact that he hadn't trialled all that well, he had told me everything I needed to know. The Whites had travelled to Rosehill to watch him trial and as soon as I dismounted I told Geoff his gelding would win the BMW Stakes. At that stage of the game, with The Diva gone, the weight-for-age ranks were a bit thin. Eremein, patched up knees and all, looked the real deal.

As a middle-distance horse with staying qualities he was always going to be found wanting at his early starts back from a spell. But his performances were still more than satisfactory. His third start back from his nine months off was the Chipping Norton Stakes where he went down by a nose to Gai Water-house's magnificent campaigner Desert War after copping a bad check at the 1000-metre mark that almost certainly cost him the race. It was a great run on Eremein's part and left me convinced that nothing would better him at his subsequent starts.

The punters knew he was coming back to his best and sent Eremein out a heavily backed favourite in the Ranvet Stakes. He didn't disappoint, winning by a length from Our Smoking Joe and Desert War. Everything was working sweetly to plan. The 2000-metre journey of the Ranvet was not his ideal dis-tance. We knew he would be much better over the 2400 metres of the BMW and were very confident he would be difficult to beat in the weight-for-age Group 1.

In a small BMW field Eremein was left further back than we might have desired. Three furlongs from home it didn't look like he was in a winning position at all. But, by then, I had figured out a certain idiosyncrasy peculiar to Eremein. At about the 600-metre mark or so, he would hit a flat spot. It looked like he was loping along but he was actually drifting through his own version of the doldrums. I would have to really work him through that part of the race. Experience told me it was only a phase and once he was through it – look out! Sure enough, he came out of his slumber like a supercharged rocket. The transition from dawdling to top gear was mind-blowing. It may have looked like he was just loping along, such was his big, powerful action, but he was fairly chewing up the ground. Over the closing stages, Eremein was devastating as he powered to an easy win.

As a horse who appreciated moving up in distance, it took a bit of a switch on the part of the Denhams to bring him back to 2000 metres for the Queen Elizabeth Stakes at Randwick. He was a highly fancied contender in a hot field and everybody expected him to win. From my perspective, the drop in distance threw a question mark into the mix. That doubt intensified when he came out of the gate with less than his usual dash. In fact, by his standards, Eremein was positively flat. Again, with three-quarters of the journey done, he went through the doldrums and I had to give him a real shake. When the out-standing mare Aqua D'Amore kicked clear, I knew we had our work cut out to reel her in. But, once again, the mighty turbocharger inside my racing machine suddenly clicked into action and Eremein went at them like an unstoppable force. He suddenly released all his pent-up energy to catapult past rival horses as if they were standing still. On that day at Randwick he smashed 'em. I was almost pinching myself in disbelief – here was a jockey who had bid his farewells to a legend just five months before and now he was on the back of the next superstar of the turf!

Eremein was a brilliant specimen and when we met again on his return for the 2006 spring carnival, he looked absolutely magnificent – bigger and stronger than ever. In my mind, he already deserved to be a raging hot favourite for the Cox Plate and the Melbourne Cup. His first run back from his spell was fantastic – better than the initial outing he'd had after his previous layoff. I was on him again for his second start of the campaign, Chelmsford at Randwick, and the improvement was immediately evident as he beat far fitter rivals for a last-stride win. Fitness-wise, he had a long way to go before nearing his best and my thoughts were that if they couldn't beat him back in autumn, then they certainly weren't going to get near him now. From my viewpoint, he had pulled up well from both of those two starts back, so it came as a real shock when Allan Denham phoned me to say: 'We've got a problem. The vets can't quite put their finger on it but he seems to be fine for days and then sore for the next two'.

We were soon to learn that this champion in the making had developed a back problem and when he did certain work it would flare up. Later, the stable would deduce that after his first two runs they had started galloping him in the anti-clockwise direction to prepare him for the spring carnival and the Melbourne way of going. Eremein wasn't used to seeing the course crossing at Rosehill while travelling in the opposite direction and had attempted to jump it. He must have landed awkwardly and damaged his back. It wasn't until the next day, when he had well and truly cooled down, that it flared up. Once again, after just two starts back, the campaign was in tatters. There would be no spring glory for Eremein. As I said, none of us can afford to dwell on the 'what ifs', but it did come as a bit of a disappointment. I had done my homework on

Eremein, taken the chance on the prospects of him returning from the knee operations and had every right to believe that once again I was in for a boom spring. But, as Sloane would remind me, I had enjoyed a magical run for the past three springs; it was time for someone else to have a turn.

As the heat of summer eased into the clear blue days of autumn 2007, Eremein made another comeback. The campaign mapped out by the Denhams was almost identical to the previous year and included the Ranvet Stakes and the BMW Stakes at Rosehill, and Queen Elizabeth Stakes at Randwick. Eremein had enjoyed a long spell and looked bigger and more powerful than ever. Once again, his first two starts back were lengths better than last time round. 'He's going to win three big ones again,' I thought to myself. His first run back had been over 1200 metres before racing in the Chipping Norton, in which he finished a very handsome fourth. Taking into account how far behind in fitness he was compared with his rivals, it was a super run. For Eremein to finish so well over the mile (1600 metres) distance was incredible at such an early stage in his preparation. Incredibly, lightning struck not twice, but thrice. Two runs back and he encountered another hurdle – this time with a hind leg which may have been a secondary injury caused by the back problem. Often when horses are sore they will compensate by putting more weight on one leg. Over time, this in turn develops into an injury. During his first two runs back the gelding had looked and felt good but there was a slight difference in his gait. When he was approaching top gear he appeared to be labouring just a bit. I had put it down to the fact that he was way short of full fitness and match practice. Then came the phone call from Allan Denham: 'He's gone again.'

A team of vets were summoned to examine him, tests were

run and re-run. But nothing showed up. The equine experts were left scratching their heads. It was a terrible shame because I had long believed that Eremein would be the real deal when it came to the 3200-metre journey of the Melbourne Cup. He was a naturally gifted stayer and if anybody thought that he was outstanding over 2400, I was convinced that he would step up and show them his true class over the longer journey. The flat spot that was customary in his performances would become less of an issue as he moved up in distance. Moreover, it meant that he had the ability to rip off really fast sectional times when it really counted – at the back end of a gruelling staying race. He was a natural for the 3200 metres. I couldn't wait to get him to the barrier on Cup day in Melbourne. And along the way would have been the Cox Plate. There was no doubt that Eremein was the best weight-for-age horse in Australia. The Plate was there for the taking. But it was never going to happen. The Chipping Norton of 2007 was the last time I would ride the gelding.

As everybody in the game knows, there is always another day, another race, another opportunity. In the post-Diva days my radar had picked up a very positive pulse about a horse in the John O'Shea stable. By Encosta De Lago out of Surrealist, Racing To Win had the mark of brilliance. Although they would both ultimately shape as potential Cox Plate contenders, Racing To Win was on a different program to Eremein, so it was possible for a jockey with a bit of luck and the right connections on his side to ride both horses in their respective campaigns.

As a young horse Racing To Win had been ridden by Hugh Bowman and had shown terrific form behind the very best of his crop, including the brilliant Paratroopers. It was clear that Racing To Win would eventually be set for the greatest mile race in Australia – the Doncaster Handicap at Randwick. But, despite his brilliance, I had reservations about the grey gelding's ability to see out the distance, particularly one as gruelling as the Doncaster, which in many ways is more like a 2000-metre race. He won a Group 2 at Hobartville on 5 March and a month later beat Paratroopers by a long head in the George Ryder Stakes over 1500 metres at Rosehill. But I was still less than convinced. The 1500 metres at Rosehill is more like a 1400-metre event anywhere else which, in my book, left it a long way short of the demanding Doncaster. On the plus side, Racing's form leading into that start had been outstanding. The gelding had certainly attracted a fan club, but I wasn't a member. Despite my great regard for John O'Shea I made it quite clear I wanted to get off Racing to score the ride on the John Hawkes–trained horse called Malcolm. My perception of Racing was that he was a great sprinter with a brilliant turn of speed but he was, at best, a seven-furlong horse – definitely not a miler. John O'Shea thought I was crazy. His view was clear-cut. 'Getting off this horse is the biggest mistake you could make,' he said. As it turned out, John Hawkes did me a monster favour. After chasing him for days, he gave me a flat no. I wouldn't be riding Malcolm. I would remain with the lightly weighted Racing To Win for the Doncaster.

With all my energy and focus now on the O'Shea charge, I concentrated on working closely as possible with John, especially during track work, to put the polish on Racing in the lead-up to the Doncaster. In those early morning sessions it became clear to me that here was a truly exceptional horse. His stable nickname was Kostya and he wore it well. A perfect gentleman out of the ring, like multiple world boxing champion Kostya Tszyu, once the battle started he was a highly focused fighting machine. He looked, felt and performed like a Doncaster winner. But I still had nagging doubts. Was he up to the gruelling Randwick distance and the unforgiving pace of the big Group 1 handicap? My time with grand gallopers Private Steer and Sprint By had shown me exactly what was needed to win the Donny. Racing was a fabulous horse and at 51 kilograms he was carrying no weight, but was he up to the standard? Experience told me that the class of the field and the handicap conditions often delivered blanket finishes, with as many as 10 horses going across the line within a few lengths of each other. In the 2006 race I knew I was on a good chance, but wasn't sure Racing would have the necessary toughness to prevail under such pressure. Bad luck can get good horses beaten, but ordinary horses don't win the best mile race in the land. They go at such a tempo in the Doncaster that it tends to suck the sprinting ability out of the more brilliant performers. That summed up my reservations about Racing as we headed for the barrier.

You are never too old to be surprised. Racing jumped well with good gate speed and relaxed beautifully to settle about fourth on the fence, just off the lead. But I knew the telling of the tale would come when the field crested the rise in the Randwick straight. Could Racing go with them? To my total surprise, just when I was expecting him to die around the 100-metre mark he was doing his best work. He finished off the race like a good thing to beat a couple of flyers in Guy Walters' Johan's Toy and the Gai Waterhouse–trained Bentley Biscuit to the line. I couldn't believe it. The horse that I had totally underestimated had delivered an absolutely stunning performance to land a third Doncaster Handicap for me. John O'Shea didn't miss me. 'I told you he could do it,' he declared with a knowing grin cracking his dial. 'You must be a bloody idiot. I don't know what got into your head to think you could get off this horse!'

It was a lesson well learnt. In one dazzling performance Racing To Win had blown all the question marks away.

That night warranted a bit of a celebration. It wasn't the Melbourne Cup, but a third Doncaster is definitely worth a toast or two. By any measure, I am no drinker, but I do enjoy the odd bottle of wine of a weekend – particularly when there is an event worth celebrating. Beer may be the great Aussie tipple but it tends to go straight to my girth.

As Racing To Win headed for a well-deserved spell to freshen up for the spring and ultimately the Cox Plate, it occurred to me that a dilemma was looming. Eremein and Racing To Win were both Cox Plate-bound and one thing was for sure – I couldn't ride both. There was no pressure on me from either the O'Shea or Denham stables. However, once again the decision was made for us when Eremein broke down. All my attention swung to Racing To Win.

The flying grey gelding looked a picture on his return in the spring of 2006. After a tough autumn the spell had done him the world of good and he was bigger and more athletic looking than ever. On 16 September he came out and won the Theo Marks Stakes at Rosehill in explosive style. In a field which included the 2005 Theo Marks winner Paratroopers, Racing showed that he was even better as a four-year-old. His performance that had the taciturn John O'Shea grinning from ear to ear. The grey gelding had been brilliant in winning the Doncaster but this was far and away his best performance as he shot past his rivals and eased down over the final stages to win by the better part of two lengths. Danny Beasley, who had a right to believe the race was his when his mount New Edge went past Paratroopers, later told reporters he couldn't believe it when Racing To Win came sailing past. I could barely believe it either and gave a spontaneous victory salute as we went past the post, earning myself a $1000 fine in the process.

The victory definitely put his rivals on notice, but the grey gelding was just gathering momentum. He backed up on 7 October to win the Roman Consul Stakes at Randwick on his way to what would prove a five-race unbeaten streak. When weights were declared for spring's big Group 1 mile at Randwick, the Epsom Handicap, Racing To Win was saddled with a hefty 57 kilograms, six more than he had carried to victory in the autumn. John O'Shea was less than impressed, telling the media that anyone with a mind for backing light-weight chances would definitely welcome the news. At that stage, Racing was no definite starter for the Epsom. John would reserve his decision until the gelding had run in the George Main Stakes over 1600 metres at Randwick the week before. With Desert War heading the challengers, the event would be an exacting test for Racing To Win. True to his name the gelding again found the post in great style to beat Red Dazzler and Desert War.

Despite the reservations John held about the Epsom weight, the gelding backed up for the big race the following week. To win the Epsom, Racing To Win would have to re-write the record books. And he did just that by starting as the shortest priced favourite in the history of the race. The warhorse, Desert War, was shooting for an Epsom hat-trick that day and might have pulled it off. But Racing To Win refused to submit to the big weight he was carrying and simply wore his rival down to win by a half-neck in a finish that had the Randwick mob on their feet. As if I needed further evidence that I had under-estimated the gallant grey back in the autumn, Malcolm, the horse that I had fancied riding in the Doncaster, was one-and-a-half lengths back in third place. In winning the Epsom, Racing joined the likes of Super Impose in becoming only the fourth horse to land the Doncaster–Epsom double and the first in 27 years to take out the George Main – Epsom double. I was in no doubt he had really treated the Randwick fans to some-thing special and had no hesitation in telling anyone, including the media throng, that they should back him for the forth-coming Cox Plate. The victory nudged Racing's record out to four Group 1 wins. From just 13 starts he had notched nine wins and four seconds. The gelding hadn't quite entered the realm of champions, but certainly looked capable of doing so. The Cox Plate couldn't come quick enough.

In six months the jockey who almost blew his chance at a long-term association with Racing To Win had gone from sceptic to convert. Now, my plan was to help the gelding realise his full potential as a racing thoroughbred. In his previous preparation leading up to the Doncaster victory, I had found him highly strung, a bit revvy, a bit overkeen and too willing to give 110 per cent in everything he did. In his preparation leading up to the Cox Plate, the plan was to make him relax, learn how to conserve his energy so that he could call on it when it really counted. At his first trial back he was cracking his neck to get right up there with the pace but I just sat on him and let him canter around behind them. The plan was to ride him quietly, just let him cruise and get used to it. He was beaten by a good 12 lengths but it didn't matter. This was a long-term project. The chance to really exert himself would come soon enough. By the time he entered the barriers for the George Main and the Epsom he was a much more relaxed horse. From the perspective of all of us involved in his preparation, Racing To Win was training to win in a less highly-strung, more mature style. We could not have been happier.

For a horse that thrived on the action, October 2006 posed a problem. It would be a three full weeks between his Epsom victory and his next start, the Cox Plate. We sent him down to Melbourne early in the month and he settled in like a local. John O'Shea had ruled out the option of starting him in the Yalumba Stakes over 2000 metres at Caulfield a fortnight before on the basis that he didn't want him running a similar distance to the Cox Plate before the big race.

Moonee Valley takes a bit of getting used to so we took Racing out there twice to get a good feel for the place. A full week before the Plate we galloped Racing on the outside of the course proper in the company of stablemate Primus over a mile, with my mount sitting about two lengths or so off the other horse and then joining in at the turn. The grey went past the post a neck or so behind Primus. As an exercise in getting him acclimatised to the course he had come through in great shape. It was a perfect scene-setter. A week later he would be truly racing to win.

The closer to race day, the better the gelding looked. At Moonee Valley Racing Club's Breakfast With The Stars he turned in an outstanding gallop, leaving nobody in doubt that he would start favourite for the Plate. All my doubts about him had totally evaporated. The gelding had developed into a lovely horse – mature, race-smart and with the preparation under his girth to run out the 2040 metres of the weight-for-age championship of Australasia.

It was a glorious spring day in Melbourne for almost everyone – except the connections of Racing To Win. We had drawn a middle barrier and my plan was to have him in the top six horses or so one length off the fence once they settled down. Racing jumped well and there was a bit of a charge on early that kept us four lengths wide off the rail. At the first opportunity I would tuck him inside closer to the rail. The chance to grab that perfect spot presented itself. I threw the anchor out to go left and grab a position that would have had us ideally placed in about fifth spot, one off the fence. Then Lisa Cropp came storming up on Miss Finland and shunted me out three deep. We were coming down the hill banking into the turn and the momentum caught Racing To Win off balance. My guess is that he tried to reach for the turf as the ground was falling away and, with his weight going forward, landed on the wrong leg. The shock shot straight up into his shoulder inflicting severe muscle damage. Our race was run. We trailed off to finish second last. He was lame and pretty distressed when I pulled him up. Everybody associated with the horse was gutted because we had been so confident. It's amazing how, in the space of a heartbeat, events can turn sour. In a split second we had gone from claiming the perfect spot in the race to being totally out of contention. While Racing To Win headed for leg scans and a long spell, I was left to survey the damage of my own spring campaign. With Eremein and now the grey gelding in the care of the vets, what had looked like another brilliant Melbourne carnival had turned to dust. As far as my Caulfield and Melbourne Cup hopes were concerned there was little in my book to set the pulse racing. As surely as the hands of good fortune had swung my way in the previous three Melbourne carnivals, they had abandoned me this time. Such is the nature of the racing game.

Instead of mourning what might have been, I set about trying to make the very best of what remained. This was the Melbourne spring carnival, the greatest time of the racing year, and I wasn't about to drop my approach to being fighting fit simply because Lady Luck had taken a holiday. When at home, I have enough fitness aids, including the kids and working around our property, to keep me fit. But being away from home was entirely different. My Melbourne routine revolved around a mobile gym called Fighting Fit. You simply called up the operators, found a pleasant part of town as a backdrop for a workout and got busy on the treadmill, bikes or walking machine. As for weights, jockeys steer clear of anything likely to pack on the muscle. Instead, I've found that boxing is a great way to enhance endurance and the type of upper body strength that all jockeys need.

A whole year had gone by but it was impossible to escape the impressions Makybe Diva had left on Melbourne. Each year past winners of the Cup are paraded around the track, but this year the mare wouldn't be there. Instead, she was happily picking at the lush grass on Tony Santic's Geelong property and, by my calculations, nine or so weeks in foal to the English Epsom Derby winner Galileo. When word had come through that the mare had returned a positive to the pregnancy test, I had paid her a visit. She'd looked a picture. In fact, she'd looked like she could have been back in work. The thought had crossed my mind that she might have retired when she was still peaking and I'd wondered whether, with proper rest and preparation, she might have returned to Flemington in the spring of 2006 for another crack at the Melbourne Cup. But then I'd reminded myself that she had retired when she was still sound and with her health intact, and now it was her time to be a mum. There was no doubt her foals would be in great demand. Earlier in 2006, Tony Santic had sold a Redoute's Choice colt out of Makybe Diva's dam Tugela for $2.5 million at the Sydney Easter yearling sale.

The breeding history showed that few progeny of Melbourne Cup winning mares ever matched the feats of their illustrious mothers. Only six mares had won the Cup in the previous 40 years. Light Fingers won in 1965 for Bart Cummings but the sum total of her progeny's record was one metropolitan win. Empire Rose delivered a couple of country performers. The brilliant Let's Elope was mated with four absolute blueblood sires in Danehill, Seeking The Gold, Danzig and Storm Cat to produce just one Group 2 winner, while Jezabeel's three unions with Danehill didn't exactly set the world alight.

The racing public couldn't have cared less about those statistics as they awaited the arrival of the Diva's first foal with the sort of expectation usually reserved for royalty, and in August 2007 she delivered a bay colt. If everything went to plan and the mare remained healthy there was no reason why she couldn't give birth to as many as a dozen foals. From the outset, the breeding industry was talking about a price tag of $2–3 million for a yearling by the great mare. Her stakes-winning days were done, but her money-making ways as a dam were just beginning. And to think that when Makybe Diva's mother Tugela was first offered for auction in foal to the stallion Desert King, she didn't attract a bid.

The timing of the thoroughbred breeding season meant that the mare would never make it back to Flemington for the parade of past winners – unless Tony decided to give her a year off. But those closest to her greatest feats would have a perpetual reminder. A life-size bronze statue stood in Port Lincoln and there was a replica planned for Flemington.

With an eye on the 2006 Melbourne Cup, all the leading jockeys had their Caulfield Cup rides well and truly locked up. The later it gets the harder it is to jump on a good one. Lloyd Williams, Victoria's legendary thoroughbred owner, punter and one of the most astute students of the game, had a very under-rated galloper by the name of Zipping heading for the spring staying events. The five-year-old gelding was a son of Danehill and, as the brother of 2004 Caulfield Cup winner Elvstroem, had plenty in his corner. The only problem was that he was a second emergency for the Caulfield Cup and looked a very remote chance of earning a start. So my services were duly booked by Kembla Grange–based trainer Gwenda Markwell who had Grand Zulu among the Caulfield runners. If Zipping somehow found his way into the field, I would revert to the Lloyd Williams–owned galloper. Sure enough, one and then two horses came out of the field. I spoke to Gwenda and she was fine about releasing me because she had Kieran McEvoy ready to ride Grand Zulu. The only problem was that the owners were not privy to this under-standing because at no stage of the game had Zipping looked a real prospect of getting a start. The owners dug in their heels. They wanted Boss on Zulu. Eventually, the stewards had to sort it out and I was allowed to revert to my preferred ride.

In the Caulfield, Zipping drew wide, got out the back door and didn't have the run of the race at all. But appearances can deceive. In fact, I thought he had run well and phoned Lloyd Williams to say, 'This horse looked like he ran an ordinary race, but if you take a look at his last 200 metres I'll bet it's one of the fastest of the race.' After being pushed way out the back, Zipping had finished off his race in great style charging into the picture in 12th place but just 4.3 lengths behind the winner. As it turned out his final furlong was the quickest of them all. My impression was that he was a real Melbourne Cup chance. Being a Danehill progeny, his ability over 3200 metres carried a question mark, but his form at Flemington had been outstanding, way better than on any other track. The only problem was that with time running out before the first Tuesday in November, he still had to qualify for the 3200-metre classic.

That small matter was rectified when Zipping ground them down to win the Moonee Valley Cup and qualify for the big one. It was a real tradesman-like effort with a fair weight on his back over 2500 metres and I reasoned that with just 52.5 kilograms in the Cup, he would be a far better chance than his 20–1 odds might indicate. In my book, he was top four material. The next phase in my Cup homework was to figure a race strategy that would suit Zipping down to the ground. So, I had Lloyd send me 15 years' worth of Melbourne Cup footage and went through them race by race until I found a winner which most closely resembled Zipping. There it was in 1999, the Bart Cummings–trained Rogan Josh with John Marshall aboard. I watched the race over and over again and made up my mind I would ride Zipping exactly like the jockey had ridden Rogan Josh. I rang Johnny Marshall a couple times and asked him what his mind-set had been going into the race. Like the 1999 winner, we would be starting from a wide barrier and carrying a similar weight. Johnny said that Bart had wanted the horse ridden nice and quiet but the rider's plan had always been to get forward. We spoke at length about what he had been doing at certain times of the race. In that race there hadn't been much speed on and Johnny reasoned that, with his light weight, it was best to be up with the front-runners. Zipping had shown that he could come from back in the field but his runs up with the front of the pack had been just as impressive. I discussed this with Lloyd Williams and he was on exactly the same page as me. We had a plan: go forward, put him in the race, get him to relax and then take our chances from there.

That's exactly how it worked out. It was like a re-run of the Rogan Josh race. The only difference was that in 1999 the horses went slower for much longer than they did in 2006 so Rogan Josh was still on a tight rein coming into the straight. In my race, they quickened at the 1000-metre mark. Zipping was starting to chase them a bit earlier than we might have wanted. At the 300-metre mark we still looked a real chance but the superior staying abilities of the Japanese pair Delta Blues and Pop Rock proved too much in the final stages. Zipping finished an extremely creditable fourth which put his connections right among the prize money and left me with a fairly satisfied feeling for having helped a quality thoroughbred realise his potential. I walked off the racecourse content in the knowledge that we couldn't possibly have done any better. Lloyd was ecstatic.

After having won two Group 1 races in Sydney early in spring, the end of the 2006 Melbourne season stood in stark contrast to the success of previous seasons. In fact, I flew back north with not a single Group 1 to my name. You might say I was licking my wounds. I had ridden well but the wheels had fallen off a couple of good ones at the wrong time. It's that amazing grey area of racing: just when you think you have the winning formula within your grasp, it evaporates. You kid yourself at times that you have it all under control but the reality is that you never do. I took comfort in the knowledge that there would be other days, other opportunities.

But 2006 was anything but a wasted year. During the southern winter I had accepted an invitation to ride in Japan and my time there gave me another perspective on the international world of racing. During my two-month stint I was especially impressed by the quality of stayers bred and raced in Japan and should not have been the least bit surprised when Japanese horses managed to place first and second in the Melbourne Cup.

Over the previous decade the Japanese had made a concerted investment in the breeding side of the industry. When I landed in Japan my hosts politely pointed out that some of the world's best stallions and broodmares stood in the country. The investment was certainly paying off with Japanese-bred horses winning all over the world. Not least among them was the magnificent stayer Deep Impact. While Makybe Diva was preparing to race into immortality in the spring of 2005, Deep Impact was making a similar impression on Japanese racing fans.

On 23 October 2005 almost 137,000 fans crammed into at Kyoto Racecourse to witness the victory of Japan's sixth Triple Crown winner, the first in 11 years and only the second to have captured the series unbeaten. Deep Impact, a Sunday Silence colt by Wind In Her Hair, started an unbackable favourite to win the Kikkasho, the final leg of the Triple Crown and make it six wins from as many starts. Like The Diva, he was the people's champion with fans snapping up T-shirts and memorabilia.

Despite an unimposing appearance and a modest price tag as a yearling, Deep Impact had shown ability from the moment he stepped onto a track. The dark bay colt had owner Makoto Kaneko sensing he had purchased something truly special when he won by four lengths on debut. He followed that with a five-lengths win. Two starts later he won the Triple Crown's first leg, Satsukisho, by two-and-half lengths, then gave his rivals a drubbing in the Japanese Derby.

I was treated to his farewell performance in Japan when he turned up at Kyoto's Hanshin track to win his fifth Group 1 race by five lengths before heading for France and the Prix de L'Arc de Triomphe. After running third in the French classic his connections said they would return the following year for another crack. But then came the news that the horse had returned a positive swab and had been stripped of his third place. Redemption came in the best way for the Japanese hero when he bounced back to win his last two starts, the Japan Cup in November and the Arima Kinen in December, before retiring to stud at the end of 2006. Among those who chased him home in the Arima Kinen were Melbourne Cup stars Pop Rock and Delta Blues.

During my time in Japan I encountered some outstanding gallopers but Deep Impact was clearly the pick. However, the Australians stand up exceedingly well when compared alongside the world's best. I have ridden in great racing centres like Hong Kong, Japan and Dubai and am certain that our top thoroughbreds can mix it with the best. Horses like Makybe Diva and Eremein could have won at Group 1 level wherever they raced. Paul Perry proved that with Choisir, Joe Janiak with Takeover Target and Lee Freedman with Miss Andretti when they campaigned successfully in England. They showed that

Australian owners and trainers should not be daunted by the prospect of taking their best horses overseas. Once upon a time, distance was a huge impediment but, these days, the world is a much smaller place.

Japan was an education in so many ways. While Australian jockeys enjoy their share of fame and publicity at carnival time, it's all year round in Japan. Top riders like Yutaka Take are feted as national superstars and attract enormous public followings and support.

Such is the spending power of the country's thoroughbred owners, not all of the best Japanese-owned horses campaign in Japan. Boom sire Fusaichi Pegasus, for instance, made his reputation in the United States after being born at Stone Farm in Kentucky.

The mighty FuPeg is a son of the great stallion Mr Prospector and was born on 12 April 1997 and purchased as a yearling for US$4 million by Fusao Sekiguchi. The youngster's name was derived from a combination of his owner's name, Fusao, and the Japanese word 'ichi', meaning No.1 or the best. Pegasus is the winged horse of Greek mythology.

FuPeg started as the favourite and duly won the 2000 Kentucky Derby. Later that year he was sold for US$60 million to begin a new career as shuttle stallion moving between the Northern and Southern hemispheres. From the outset he was a success as a stallion. Among his Southern Hemisphere progeny would be an athletic colt by the name of Haradasun. Our paths were destined to cross, but more about that later.

While in Japan I had the honour of riding the 2005 champion two-year-old Fusaichi Richard. Owned by Fusao Sekiguchi of FuPeg fame, the grey colt was the son of champion Kurofune out of the champion mare Fusaichi Airedale. I rode him in track work for a couple of weeks and he really impressed me. A big, strong three-year-old, he was a little fierce in his work when I first encountered him so my intention was to get him to relax. The effort was worthwhile because after indifferent form in the early stages of the year, he found his groove.

As for the real business – race riding – I enjoyed it immensely. During my time in Japan I found it easier than at home and averaged a winner per meeting. In Australia, race riding is very tactical, very competitive, and jockeys ask for and give no quarter. Whereas the onus for Aussie jockeys is to get near as possible to the fence, Japanese riders aren't so bothered, being just as content to sit three or four wide for the duration. Instead of finding a position on the fence, they're more concerned with assisting the horse to find its rhythm. Japanese race pundits have a rather unflattering view of our tactical approach. They can't see why so many races in Australia are sit-and-sprint affairs. In Japan, the opposite applies. During my time there I don't think I rode in a single slowly run race. Every race is run at a solid tempo which means the fields are more strung out and there is less chance of interference.

They say travel broadens the mind. As short as it was, my winter in Japan added plenty to my racing education.

23

A thunderbolt . . .
wearing L-plates

When you are on a good thing, why change? That was John O'Shea's approach as he laid out a carbon copy of Racing To Win's previous autumn campaign. The grey was on his way back from the injury incurred in the Cox Plate and there seemed no reason to think that the star of 2006 would not come up as big and bold as ever for 2007. He was working well and doing everything right with the willingness and enthusiasm we had come to know of him. But . . .

Something was not quite right.

Thoroughbreds are finely tuned animals. If you run a colt too much when he is sore, chances are he will stop running pretty quickly. Mares, on the other hand, have a much higher pain threshold. Maybe geldings fall somewhere in between. As Racing To Win attempted to put his severe injury behind him and return to what made him a true star of the turf, the grey wasn't 100 per cent. It was only a tiny degree or two, but John sensed it. Although he had been spelled, it isn't very long from the end of spring to the start of another autumn racing season. The decision was made to turn him out for a longer rest.

Late February found me back in Melbourne to ride Press The Button for David Hayes in the Blue Diamond Stakes at Caulfield. On the same card was Haradasun, the brilliantly bred colt with the headline-grabbing price tag. The son of Fusaichi Pegasus was a hot favourite for the Schweppervescence Cup but, with Nash Rawiller aboard, produced an erratic effort that cost him the race. From my viewpoint, the colt was wayward, brilliant and looked a real challenge for any jockey. It was the sort of challenge I couldn't resist. In spite of his wayward nature, he had posted similar form as Racing To Win the year before. My calculation was that he would attract a weight of 51 or 52 kilograms heading into the autumn Group 1 races. I knew Nash couldn't ride that low. Making a mental note to talk to his trainer, Tony Vasil, at the first opportunity, I headed for Tullamarine and my return flight to Sydney. Chance is a fine thing. There, at the airport bar sipping on a beer by himself, was the trainer of Haradasun.

I walked up to him, sat down and said, 'That horse, he's only gunna get 51 and . . .'

I didn't get to finish the sentence. Tony Vasil took a short pull on his beer and said, 'Done deal.'

There was no doubt Haradasun had talent and the ability to be a genuine star of the turf, but he was wayward. He was running great sectional times but still finding ways to lose races. With no disrespect to Nash, my guess was that he needed to be ridden like a racehorse rather than the superstar everybody assumed him to be.

Once again, I had cause to thank my genes and the pride

I took in trying to retain a good bodyweight without resorting to fasting. I've always been comfortable at 51–53 kilograms. Plenty of jockeys blow out to 56 or so and they have to work hard to strip off the kilos. I've never been one for the sauna, except when I'm riding in one of the big carnivals when I might be called on to ride lighter than usual. One of my best household investments was a big therapeutic spa that not only soothed aching joints, muscles and trouble spots like my lower back, but helped shed the odd kilo when needed.

My first race ride on Haradasun was in the George Ryder Stakes at Rosehill after the colt had landed in Sydney. It was a small field but with gallopers like Apache Cat to contend with, there was a bit of quality about. The horses went slow early and he was last into the straight as the leaders sprinted for home. I was carrying the whip in my right hand and when I gave him a reminder, he shied away a bit. As if spotting something in the crowd he started to veer right. Yet, despite heading off at an angle, he was still travelling quicker than his opponents and motored past Mentality and Apache Cat to grab the lead and win his first Group 1. He had done everything wrong by almost running off the track but Haradasun still had beaten a quality field. It was a devastating performance, particularly taking into account that he would be heading into the Doncaster with 3 kilos less than he carried in the Ryder. History showed the up-and-coming three-year-olds with light weights were very hard to beat in autumn.

Haradasun was still trying ways to lose a race but I just put it down to him being an immature colt. Fusaichi Pegasus progeny were known as late developers. Later, when he went for a spell at the end of autumn, the chiropractors discovered that his neck and back were out of alignment. It was possible that he was running away from pain. When he wasn't being asked for a great effort, Haradasun would run straight and true. But under real pressure he wanted to spear to the left. In Melbourne that meant heading towards the rail whereas in Sydney he would want to run off the track. Some horses would shy irrespective which direction they were travelling. But this horse always went left which made me think that the chiropractors were ultimately on the right track because he certainly looked to be attempting to gallop away from whatever caused him discomfort.

At the time though I figured he was still finding his feet with the Sydney way of going and was pretty confident that there would be no repeat in the Doncaster. It was a stroke of good fortune when we drew the inside barrier. Following the rail and having horses outside him would definitely be a big advantage. This time, I made a mental note to carry the whip in my left hand.

In so many ways Haradasun fitted the bill for the big Randwick race – light weight, right age, brilliant turn of acceleration, lightly raced, a natural athlete chock full of talent. Whereas Racing To Win knew exactly where he needed to be at any given time and had a very amenable, almost push-button, manner, Haradasun was not nearly so tractable. But, boy, was he an athlete. He just oozed class. Very few horses give you the goose bumps the second you jump on their backs. This fella had the magic. The first time I rode him, the trip to the barrier felt like floating on a cloud of air. Whenever he put a hoof down it was as if it didn't even touch the ground. Makybe Diva had a lovely smooth action, but this fella was different again – so light on his feet he was almost cat-like. If he could behave himself, we were justifiably confident about his chances.

With just eight starts to his name the least experienced horse in the Doncaster started as the favourite. Unlike the Ryder, my plan was to fire him out and have him right in front with the leaders. He was screaming to be ridden like that. He bounced out of the barrier and settled into third on the fence. We came smoking over the rise and when I let him go he went sideways again. However, that didn't stop him. Apache Cat, with a great turn of speed, led in the straight but Haradasun caught him about 200 metres from home. The challenges were coming but nothing was going to catch the colt as he saluted the judge ahead of Mentality and Divine Madonna. It was my fourth Doncaster victory and my third in just four years. But, more importantly, I had done it on a horse whose talent was so scary that almost nothing seemed beyond him. If he ran straight he would win by five lengths. To think, at that stage of his racing career, the colt was still learning the business. He was still wearing L-plates.

It was especially pleasing to see Tony Vasil step up to the podium to accept his rewards as the winning trainer. As he told the crowd he had been under more pressure to train the $25 million blueblood colt than any other horse in his entire career, so the victory meant everything to him. Tony had worked tirelessly to overcome Haradasun's hoof problems. The hard work and sleepless nights had paid off. Now, with a slashing win in the Doncaster under his belt, the colt's reputation as a racing thoroughbred and, eventually, a sire with a massive price tag, seemed assured.

Haradasun's next start was to be the Queen Elizabeth and with the colt certain to carry more than the miserly 53 kilograms he humped in the Donny, Nash Rawiller was back on board. It was billed as a match race between the seasoned Desert War and the new kid on the block. Desert War, Coalesce and Grand Zulu cleared out on the pack with the favourite Haradasun heading the rest. There was no value in giving Desert War a start and hoping to run him down. He would simply hold you at bay. Getting to him wasn't the problem. But getting past him was a different matter altogether. The best tactic was to sit on him and then swoop at the right moment and hold on to the lead for dear life.

Haradasun had the brilliance to do that but in the Queen Elizabeth he had two factors against him. The first was that he had spotted Desert War too great a start. The second was that when Nash did wind him up, the colt again ran erratically under pressure. The connections were disappointed with Haradasun's return to his old ways but I knew they didn't have too much cause for concern. There would be other days for the brilliant colt.

24

Have saddle will travel

In my quiet moments when I sat down to analyse my career, it became evident that my finest times were the products of the greatest pressure. This realisation reminds me of the importance of guarding against complacency. When something becomes routine it can develop into a habit and before long that habit has become a rut.

At no stage of my life had that happened to me. My instinct to change things averted it. Instead of avoiding pressure and settling for the soft option, I had always gone looking for a greater challenge. Gympie to the Gold Coast, Gold Coast to Brisbane, Brisbane to Sydney, setting a deadline to return from the neck injury, being part of the campaign to turn The Diva into a weight-for-age champion. All of those events presented a challenge and came with more than a measure of pressure.

The warm afterglow of those three Melbourne Cup victories would only sustain me for so long. By the time 2007 had rolled around, I could feel the old familiar itch. It was time to change things again.

In so many ways, Sloane and I had achieved everything we could have wished for. Great family life, two beautiful kids and a terrific home in Sydney. We had built the sort of existence others might envy.

But beyond the comfort and the familiarity, I could see that a routine had developed around my life as a jockey. Because I have never been attached for any length of time to a leading stable, the prospects of winning premierships were slim. Instead, my attention had been focused on establishing myself as the leading winner of Group 1 events. To do that, my attentions fell very much on the spring and autumn carnivals. The rest of the year, in a few respects, was just like marking time. And life was too short and precious for marking time.

We decided to go to Hong Kong – Dad, Mum, kids and the dogs. The whole shooting match. In some ways it was a new challenge and unfinished business. My first contract with the Hong Kong Jockey Club some years before had offered a fabulous time and a thrilling change of scene for a young Australian couple who had seen little of the world outside of Australia. And I had been the wide-eyed kid in a strange new world. As far as the racing was concerned, I hadn't done myself full credit. At no stage had I felt on top of my game.

This time it would be different. I was older, more experienced and, hopefully, a bit smarter. Knowing the lay of the land would make an enormous difference. Hong Kong's racing environment demands total attention from its participants. You can't afford to be distracted. The second time round there would be no protracted settling-in period. From day one it would be pure business.

That said, my priorities would always be family first. My commitment to racing and career would always be top shelf, but if I realised that my family wasn't thriving outside of Australia, I would have no hesitation in coming home. It certainly helped that Sloane sincerely enjoyed the Hong Kong lifestyle and felt right at home with the culture, pace and challenge of the city.

As for the kids, it would be quite a contrast from the space and quiet of our family home on a generous acreage with bushland views on the outskirts of Sydney to a high-rise apartment above the hustle and bustle of one of the world's busiest cities. My hopes were that Tayte and Carter would learn a different language, adapt to and appreciate a new culture and use the experience as part of their education. In so many ways it would open their eyes to the world outside of Australia. From a family perspective, Hong Kong is a relatively safe city. Compared to many other places, law and order does not occupy too much space in the local media. Sloane and I have always felt safe there.

Only jockeys considered to be at the top of their craft are issued invitations by the Hong Kong Jockey Club. When you consider that riders from all around the world leap at the opportunity to work there, it is certainly a privilege that you cannot afford to take lightly. As a provider for my family I also knew that Hong Kong's favourable taxation climate would help maximise my earnings.

All expatriates make sacrifices when leaving a country as fantastic as Australia in order to work overseas. One compensation is that Hong Kong has a lively Australian community and Aussies always know how to have fun. It goes without saying that you miss friends, family, the weather, beaches and

Australia's easy-going outdoor lifestyle. That's why it is important to appreciate what a place like Hong Kong has to offer: a rich diversity of cultures, modern amenities and first-class schools. Knowing that you won't be there forever helps remind you to make the most of it. And the shopping is unbelievable. Everything your heart desires, including Australian wine, is available for sale.

It also helps knowing that Australia is only eight hours flying time away. That makes it relatively easy to dash back home, especially if there is the prospect of riding a potential winner in a glamour event like the Melbourne Cup.

The opportunity to ride in Hong Kong again came along at the right time for me. At the completion of the 2006 spring carnival I was heading into my 37th year. Jockeys' careers may run a good few years longer than the average athlete, but you can't argue with time. At the most, I had eight good years left. Somewhere in the early part of that period, I was bound to hit my peak. My thinking was to get to Hong Kong as I was approaching the stage of my riding life where strength and athleticism intersect with experience. That's when a jockey is at his very best. With a concerted effort over the best years left to me, I could generate the sort of income and success to set my family up for life. Yes, it would be about my desire to fulfil my potential as a jockey. But one happy by-product of that endeavour would be guaranteeing my family's financial future.

However, it would mean changing my focus to a large degree. Whereas my purpose in Australia had been to build a reputation as the bloke with the ability to deliver the Group 1 wins, there are not so many opportunities in that area in Hong Kong. Instead, I would be looking to land a jockey's premiership for most wins in a season, possibly within three or four years. I knew it would be one of the hardest goals I had set myself. Hong Kong is a very intense racing scene, the punters are extremely well educated and the focus on jockeys, trainers, owners and officials is absolutely white hot. But it was exactly the challenge I needed. In Hong Kong, the pressure is constant. And that's what gets me going. The greater the pressure the better I function. As a competitor, I feed off that buzz. Spring and autumn carnivals are magical times, but they weren't enough. I needed to feel that level of expectation every day of my riding life.

In Hong Kong every race carries its own pressure. It could be a 50–1 shot in a humble Class 6 event but, such is the racing environment and the level of interest, jockeys know they are under the microscope in every race they ride. The level of scrutiny from stewards is very intense and you are expected to give your best in every race you ride. No excuses. Perform at 80 per cent of your ability and you will soon be told to go home. Every rider is contracted to the Hong Kong Jockey Club. If you don't perform, you're out the door. The newcomer landing in Hong Kong finds that he is up against some of the very best jockeys in the world. He may have been a king pin in his own country but he will receive no favours at his new workplace. In fact, he will be obliged to start at the bottom and prove himself all over again. And, unlike Australia, he will be required to ride track work every day. Trust me, it's no holiday. But that's the sort of pressure that brings out the best in me.

An application to ride in Hong Kong was lodged, the Hong Kong Jockey Club committee considered that application and took a good, hard look at my record. Nothing is a given. The club has a quota of foreign jockeys and in any one year there may be as few as two positions available. As accomplished as

I might have been, the club might easily decide to engage a young, up-and-coming rider instead of a seasoned hand. Fortunately, they gave me the green light.

It was exactly what we wanted and needed. Once the decision was made, the old adrenalin started pumping again. No matter what we do in life, all of us need to be continually reaching above ourselves, redefining our goals. The plan involved turning our family home over to friends for an indefinite period, packing up the necessities and shipping out to our new home. Our departure date was August 2007. My next commitment in Australia would have me flying south for a return visit around Melbourne Cup time.

Don't be fooled by appearances. There may be room for just one of us up there on the back of a thoroughbred, but in so many ways the Boss business has been all about the perfect partnership. Flying solo works for some folks, but nothing beats the shared experience and, since I first met Sloane all those years ago on the Gold Coast, I have managed to share the very best and worst and everything else in between with the love of my life.

Our greatest accomplishments are our two children, Tayte and Carter. You could say that they have been along for the ride as well – with certain reservations. While their dad has lived way too much of his life in the public spotlight, we have been very mindful to allow our kids to have as normal an upbringing as possible and that has meant keeping them away from the public gaze. Yet, in so many ways they have been there with us. My memories of winning that Slipper on Flying Spur are more joyous for the fact that Sloane was only a couple of months away from giving birth to Tayte. He arrived in the world on 1 June 1995.

As for names, we settled on Tayte Jackson for our first born. For one reason or another, when he was born he reminded us of our *Little Man Tate*, the 1991 movie about a child prodigy. Tayte Jackson Boss – TJ.

We always knew that we would have more than one. However, we thought that we would let Tayte achieve a measure of independence before bringing another little Boss into the world. So, four weeks after Tayte turned five, his baby sister Carter arrived on 28 June 2000. Sloane had been pregnant with Carter Rae when we were in Hong Kong but, like her brother, our precious daughter was born in Sydney.

Tayte is very much like his mum – always considered, extremely thoughtful. Whenever Sloane or Tayte undertake anything, they will think through all the angles beforehand. As for Carter, she has my impulsiveness. She is very spontaneous. When I was a kid I would run through a wall and think about just how much it hurt after the event. Carter is very much like that.

One trait Tayte has inherited from me is his ability to work by himself and be happy. I was a bit of a loner as a kid and our son has picked up on that. He quite enjoys his own company, especially when he has a project. He can go to his room and keep himself busy for hours. Carter is the opposite; she loves being around me when I am working and will drive you crazy with a million questions.

As a parent you catch yourself at times wondering just what life will deliver for your kids. I'm a great believer in the traditional values of respect and courtesy. One day, when they are old enough, they will make their own choices about the directions they will take in life. Until then, we try to give them the best support and guidance so when that time comes they will have the best chance of pulling the right rein.

Carter took to school like a duckling to a pond. Tayte has been a bit like his dad – steady without setting the honours board alight. He loves his sport and my thinking is to give him the opportunity to try as many as his heart desires until he finds the one he loves the most. As for horses, at time of writing, he has shown no real interest and that doesn't worry me one bit. Perhaps one Boss is more than enough for the racing game. Like me, when he finds something he really loves, he will latch on. I stumbled through cricket, rugby league and athletics until racing grabbed me.

Whatever choices they ultimately make in life, one quality I would love them to inherit is the value of giving every endeavour 100 per cent. I want them to respect that old adage: If it's worth doing, it's worth doing well. In imparting that wisdom, it is important to deliver it in a practical way. I'd hate my kids to see me as an over-bearing dad always pushing, pushing. In fact, I'd rather not say anything rather than run the risk of pushing them away. For that reason, as much as Tayte loves sport, I will never coach him. Instead, if he hits a good shot in tennis, I will give him encouragement, but would never try to coach or criticise. I would much rather the kids worked it out for themselves. Ideally, they learn to use their own initiative and when it comes to the time when they have to step out in the real world on their own, they will be able to cope. If a kid works it out for himself the lesson is a hundred times more powerful. As parents, we have the temptation of handing it to them on a plate, but it doesn't teach them independence. Instead, they become lazy. When it comes time for them to do it themselves, they have no idea.

Sometimes, I wonder whether I'm too harsh. The kids come to me with a problem and I invite them to work it out for themselves. I guess it says much about my own upbringing. In so many ways I had to stumble through on my own account and do it wrong a hundred times before I learned to do it right. The old value of learning by your mistakes still holds true in the Boss household.

And so it goes.

Is there any other business so focused on what happens next? Most other sports have the entire off-season to reflect on past glories. But racing goes on and on. There is always the next carnival, the next race. Everything in racing is in front of you – out there, down the track, between the horse's ears. Don't look back – you'll miss that vital split, that opening or opportunity.

So, in writing this book, I have committed one of racing's cardinal sins – spending too long looking back. Just a glance, but too long. If you've made it this far, thanks for sharing the ride. But now it's time to get back to work.

The moment, so many years ago, when that boy stepped from his grandmother's car at Gympie races and fell in love with the indefinable magic of thoroughbreds in full flight, was the turning point. It could have been a passing phase, a teenage fad soon abandoned. But it wasn't. Instead, it's been a love affair – a love affair destined to last a lifetime.

And it ain't over yet.

The best horses I have ridden

A jockey's career is a non-stop process of jumping on and off horses. From skinny-legged bush maidens at dust-blown country tracks to the blue bloods of the big city carnivals, there are so many that they could simply merge into the one nameless parade of horseflesh.

The reason they don't is that every now and then a galloper comes along who commands your attention and respect, a fair dinkum equine athlete with the personality and courage that sets it apart from the rest.

Believe me, it is easy to fall in love with such a horse. Makybe Diva was such an animal. And there are others. The statisticians can come up with all sorts of systems and ratings to rank one horse above or below another. But it would be wrong of me to impose a ranking system on the bunch selected here. Each, in his or her own way, was exceptional.

SHOGUN LODGE 1998–2003 (by Grand Lodge out of Pride Of Tahnee) was trained by Bob Thomsen and ridden by Shane Dye as a three-year-old until the jockey took up an offer to ride in Hong Kong. The first time I rode Shogun Lodge he was just four years old. I can remember jumping up on him for a track-work session at Randwick and being taken by his amazing presence and athletic physique. A new jockey on his back made no difference to him; he just went about his work in a totally unflappable way like good horses do.

Straightaway I knew he was an outstanding horse. He would constantly run exceptional training times that would have the clockers looking twice at their watches. He seemed to do it without any effort. Shogun Lodge was an easy horse to like. He was a real personality – full of energy, bubbly and honest and he remained that way right throughout his career. Whatever you asked of him he would give his best.

I won three Group 1 and a couple of Group 2 races on him but he'll be forever remembered as the horse who finished second in half-a-dozen Group 1 races. I think the reason for this was that as a two-year-old he had been taught to get well back in the field and come from behind to finish strongly. But as he matured that racing style didn't permit him to win as many races as he should have. He was then faced with the prospect of having to run 33 seconds for the final 600 metres. More often than not he would produce that sort of effort, but when you're running against the likes of Sunline and Octagonal it was diffi-cult to give them massive starts and run them down. So many times he was pipped by a nose or a short half-head.

Shogun Lodge met Sunline in the Doncaster of 2002, with both horses carrying equal weights. He gave the field a massive start, got knocked down early, picked himself up and then chased them. He lost by the barest of margins. He never knew when he was beaten. It's part of racing lore that he never made it to old age. Like the great fighter he was he died in the ring after collapsing in the Emirates Stakes at Flemington in 2003. It broke my heart because such a great old warrior deserved to spend his retirement in the paddock enjoying himself. Instead, he died on the track giving it his all.

PRIVATE STEER 2002–2004 (by Danehill Dancer out of Lishwenowen). It was wonderful to see a promising filly develop into a great racing mare. She already had an impressive reputation when John O'Shea asked me to ride her in the Stradbroke Handicap in 2003. I knew she had been winning her races in fine style so I took it upon myself to get down to the 48.5 kilograms for her Group 1 debut. Private Steer won the Stradbroke and it marked the start of a great partnership.

When I first rode her she was long and lean and all raw potential, but she quickly developed into a big racing machine with a tonne of speed. As the seasons rolled on she had more than the odd brush with injury but John was able to manage most of her setbacks. Firm tracks could really play havoc with her feet so we saw the best of her when there was a bit of give in the ground.

Her win in the Doncaster in 2004 will go down as one of the best of all time. Her trainer had her absolutely peaking for the race and, as she was favourite, we were pretty confident. We were hoping for a comfortable victory but it sure didn't turn out that way. She drew a bad barrier and then got mixed up in two really bad bits of interference before the 1000-metre mark. I could picture John in the stands tearing his hair out and saying, 'What's going on, Bossy?'

The plan had been to have her in the first eight horses, instead we were about 18th. But I reminded myself to stay calm, trust her ability and ride for luck. She was a chaser and I knew that if she had to run eight seconds for a furlong to beat another horse she would bust a gut trying to do it. She gave Grand Armee a massive start, came from an impossible position and ended up beating him soundly.

Sadly, Private Steer was retired early after being kicked in the hock by a stablemate when she was favourite for the Cox Plate. It was a real blow to me because, after that Doncaster victory in the autumn, I was convinced she would have been very hard to beat.

REPUBLIC LASS 2001–2003 (by Canny Lad out of Swift Seasons). Trained by Guy Walter. I owe plenty to this amazing filly because Guy gave me the opportunity to ride her early in her development and the three of us – trainer, jockey and filly – worked together to mould an outstanding racehorse. She never did anything wrong in track work but, at the same time, she had a mind of her own and could be very aggressive and strong-willed. On race day she was a pleasure to ride because you knew when you pushed the buttons she would give you everything she had. Before a bowed tendon cut short her career, she stamped herself as a truly great mare. In 2002 she stepped up in class to blow them away in the Adrian Knox and then a week later ran away with the Oaks. That was an amazing victory: she got mid-field and, when the split appeared, simply blew the rest of the field away. Then she met Northerly in the Ranvet in 2003, eye-balled him at the 200-metre mark and they lay all over each other for the last 100 metres in a real ding-dong battle. She was so tenacious and aggressive that she simply refused to let him pass her. That was a great victory because Northerly was one of the great champions and he'd never been beaten like that.

Republic Lass would have been favourite for the Caulfield – Melbourne Cup double the following year but she succumbed to injury. Guy didn't think twice about the decision to retire her.

SKY HEIGHTS 1998–2002 (by Zabeel out of Moet Heights) was trained by Colin Alderson at Cranbourne. I caught sight of this rangy young galloper finishing just behind the early three-year-olds in the Melbourne spring carnival. He looked like a big, skinny coat hanger and my impression was that the gelding would show his true potential once he filled out. I thought that he would be the real deal come the following autumn carnival in Sydney, so I gave Colin a call.

Coming into that campaign Sky Heights was impressive in a few lead-up runs in Melbourne but it wasn't until he landed in Sydney that he gave us a glimpse of what he could do. From spring to autumn he had grown into a big, bold front-running machine. He came out in the Rosehill Guineas in 1999 where he charged to the front and fought off every challenge thrown at him. After that run I knew he was a special for the AJC Derby because he was still improving. Again, he dictated from the front and although the rest of the field came at him in the straight, his staying ability shone through. At that stage of my career it was a real thrill because Sky Heights endorsed my faith in him and my ability to judge horseflesh.

Sky Heights then won the Yalumba Stakes at Caulfield in the spring of 2000 in a real show of courage. We drew a bad barrier and didn't start at all well and I had to ride him aggressively up the hill. Next thing you know he hit the front.

From there he just ground them into the turf with his ability to maintain a fast pace.

Sky Heights was the favourite for the Cox Plate in 2000 and I was pretty convinced that he would get the job done. But bad luck intervened. As he was due to race in Dubai later in the year he had been inoculated but had an adverse reaction to the inoculation. He appeared to have beaten it by Cox Plate day but something was amiss. Typical of Zabeel progeny he used to get a bit agitated and hot before a race and I would have to spend some time talking him down. But on this day he was unusually quiet. Alarm bells went off in my head. He cantered around to the barriers like an old dog and ended up getting beaten by about 12 lengths. But that run was hardly typical of the galloper who had won the 1999 Caulfield Cup for Damien Oliver while I was in Hong Kong.

In 2001 Sky Heights' successes included the AJC St Leger, the Sandown Classic plus a narrow second to Ethereal in the Caulfield Cup.

STARCRAFT 2002–2006 (by Soviet Star out of Flying Floozie) was one of the biggest horses I've ever ridden, a giant of a stallion, a superb athlete, beautifully balanced with a striking physique. When he walked into an enclosure everybody would stop and stare at this liver chestnut. What a specimen! By the time he went to stud in 2006, his record would show that he raced 22 times on 14 different tracks around the world for 11 wins, five of them at Group 1 level. He was foaled in New Zealand, auctioned as a yearling to a partnership headed by Australian Paul Makin and trained on the Gold Coast by Gary Newham.

He was a three-year-old the first time I rode him, taking on the older horses in the Chipping Norton Stakes on a bog of a track. He just ploughed through the soft going for a great win. I was pretty impressed so I had a chat with Gary Newham, who is an old friend of mine, about Starcraft's prospects. As a consequence I had a bit to do with his preparation heading into the AJC Derby.

I had a sneaking impression that he wasn't a natural stayer, a factor that would be proven later in his career. But, nonetheless, I was still pretty confident about his chances in the Derby. As with most three-year-old Derby hopes, the race doesn't necessarily go to the best stayer but the horse who can sprint at the end. Starcraft drew a good barrier and started well, the splits came at the right time and, although he looked gone at the last furlong, he found a little bit more under pressure and hung on to win.

Paul Makin decided on a New Zealand campaign for the horse and I rode Starcraft into second place in the Group 1 Kelt Capital Stakes over 1600 metres at Hawkes Bay. He was a highly strung colt who could easily get distracted by the crowd and lose the plot. That's what happened at Hawkes Bay.

I then had the choice between Private Steer and Starcraft for the 2004 Cox Plate but the decision was made for me when Private Steer had to be retired. The plan was to start Starcraft in the Yalumba Stakes and get him to relax before the Cox Plate. Despite having just flown home from New Zealand, he settled down well and ran third. The run had Cox Plate winner written all over it. But then we struck problems. Starcraft had been experiencing a bit of trouble with his shoulders, which we were managing, but it was not the sort of issue he needed to be carrying into a Group 1 race. He ran his heart out to finish third but, on the day, I had the impression he just wasn't his normal self.

That was when he and I parted company. His next preparation took him off to England and Europe where he won the 1600-metre Prix du Moulin at Longchamp in France before proving he was Europe's best miler by winning the Group 1 Queen Elizabeth II Stakes, which was held at Newmarket while Ascot was being refurbished.

You know when you are on a great horse the first time you ride it. As his career record would show, Starcraft was world-class. If his stud progeny look anything like their dad, they will sell well, that's for sure.

FASTNET ROCK 2003–2005 was unbelievably well bred. By Danehill out of Piccadilly Circus, he was owned by Coolmore Stud and trained by Paul Perry. I was so lucky to be associated with this horse. Although he never won as a two-year-old, he had good form heading into the Golden Slipper in 2004 and I rang Paul and asked if he would consider putting me on him. Paul agreed and Fastnet Rock ran magnificently in his next race.

He drew well in the Slipper, jumped beautifully and gave himself every opportunity. But, he was probably suffering from sore shins because of his immaturity and he couldn't go on with it. But I knew he would be develop into a magnificent horse and, come the following autumn, he could be the best sprinting three-year-old in Australia. I prayed that Paul and Coolmore would give me the chance to ride him again. Thankfully, they stuck with me.

In February 2005 Fastnet Rock chased Alinghi down to win the Lightning Stakes and then came out to win the Oakleigh Plate at Caulfield. The Newmarket at Flemington was the third leg of the sprint triple crown but the 3.5 kilograms he had to concede to Alinghi was too much and he was just beaten.

I was set to ride him in England in the Group 1 Golden Jubilee Stakes and the July Cup. But he came down with travel sickness and was returned to Australia where the decision was made to retire him to stud. It was a real shame because I felt that he was developing in the mould of the great Schillaci, the champion sprinter of the 1990s. The Rock had a splendid demeanour, was amazingly strong and well-balanced and came with a beautiful racing action. He was all class. We had a glimpse of his greatness, but never saw the best of him. He will make a super sire.

CHOISIR 2001–2003 (by Danehill Dancer out of Great Selection) was also trained by Paul Perry and aptly named. Choisir is French for 'choose', 'select' or 'to pick out' and what a choice he proved to be. He arrived on the scene a year before Fastnet Rock. After watching Choisir run in the Golden Slipper I rang Paul and drove him mad begging to ride him in his campaign as a three-year-old. Paul didn't agree straightaway. I studied Choisir a bit more and noticed that his riders seemed to be fighting him throughout the race. The big colt just wanted to run. I rang Paul again and said, 'I think I know how to ride this bloke.' Paul then gave me a chance.

We didn't win first up but I learned a lot about him. All the way to the barrier we staged a battle of wills. He was an arrogant colt and if you fought him he would just switch off. But if you went with him and let him have his way to a certain degree, he would show his better side.

I was on him for a truly memorable win in the Lightning Stakes down the Flemington straight. Because of the soft track conditions 12 of the 13 runners came to the outside. I figured that the going would be better on the inside, so Choisir and

I were on our lonesome. That didn't worry him. He was a free-running colt who didn't need other horses around him and I knew he could run under 11 seconds per furlong. I would have looked stupid if we were beaten but I had confidence in my decision and I believed in the horse. I haven't seen it before or since – where someone has gone it alone down the straight in a Group 1 race and won.

He stumbled out of the barrier on a soft track in the Oakleigh Plate at Caulfield, but managed to flash home to grab a place. My feeling was that he would win the Newmarket but the decision was made to run him in the Futurity before that. Choisir delivered another mighty performance but I think the run flattened him as he wasn't the same horse in the Newmarket. He ran his heart out but the spark was gone.

When the owners made the decision to take him to England, I fully endorsed the call to put a local jockey on him. Overseas riders competing in Australia often don't get it right. I knew the reverse could apply.

With Johnny Murtagh aboard, the Broadmeadow speed-freak rewrote history by winning twice in the same week at the Royal Ascot carnival. He backed up from the Tuesday's King's Stand Stakes with a victory in the Golden Jubilee on the Saturday, breaking the 1200-metre track record in the process.

FLYING SPUR 1994–1996 (by Danehill out of Rolls) was never a through-and-through champ like some of the others, but he holds a very special place in my career. He was super-bred and would go on to become an outstanding sire himself. But I'll always remember him because he gave me my first Group 1 win and kicked off my association with Lee Freedman. As I've described earlier, the Golden Slipper ride came about courtesy of the Jockey Tapes controversy. As luck would have it, I didn't have a ride going in to the race, was a late replacement for Jim Cassidy and ended up riding the winner. As a two-year-old he was a magnificent looking animal with perfect proportions. But he was a bit of a thinking colt and he could have his off days. He was put out in the paddock for a rest after the Sires Produce Stakes but he did so well and developed so much that the decision was made to bring him back in and run him in the 1995 Slipper. It was a masterstroke because he was very fresh. On the day, he looked fantastic with the special glow in the coat. As I've related, Lee reckoned he'd do one of two things: win or run last. It was a hot field including Octagonal so I didn't know what to think. Yet, on the way to the barrier he moved like a true athlete – he had a fantastic action like he was floating. He felt that good I couldn't help myself from telling another jockey that Flying Spur would win. We drew the inside barrier which had been a bit of a Slipper hoodoo because of the tendency to get squeezed up. But he settled well and we claimed a good mid-field position. When the splits came he chased hard to grab a terrific win.

Although I rode him a few more times, I didn't have a long association with Flying Spur. He was a bit hot and cold but possessed so much talent. The long-term blessing is that he turned into a sensational sire and I've since ridden many winners that are the product of Flying Spur. As the galloper who helped kickstart my career, he'll always hold a special place in my heart.

JUGGLER 1993–1999 (by Jugah out of Kashalyn) was an athletic gelding with the quality of a superstar. Trained by Gai Waterhouse he had an amazing disposition – every time he turned up at the track he was ready to race. Towards the end of his career he had plenty of injury niggles and woes, but, come race day, the adrenalin kicked in and he would be ready to go. He would fight past the pain and run through it. In that way he was the absolute professional and a pleasure to ride.

Blessed with a brilliant turn of speed he won four Group races and collected the cash in another eight Group and listed races before eventually retiring as an eight-year-old. I'm proud to say I was on him for plenty of those starts, including his victory in the 1996 George Main Stakes. Octagonal beat us in the 1996 Australian Cup when I probably got a bit itchy and went too soon.

We went to Dubai together where Juggler produced a magnificent sixth in the World Cup against some of the best gallopers on the planet over 2000 metres. He had never run on the dirt before but he really acquitted himself well. Throughout his career Juggler struck some of the best weight-for-age horses of modern times, but he didn't worry about their reputations – he was too busy giving his best.

SPRINT BY 1994–1997 (by Kaapstaad out of Brookes Cross) was trained by Gai Waterhouse and is one of my all-time favourite horses. I was on him riding track work before his very first start and my thoughts were that this horse was going to be a very special talent. In a maiden at Hawkesbury he was almost smashed through the fence on two occasions but he picked himself up and just blew the field away. It was amazing. After the races I jumped on the phone to Gai and said, 'This horse will win a Doncaster.' And that's exactly what he did. He went through the grades until he won the big Group 1 at Randwick in 1996.

Whether on race day or just doing track work, Sprint By was

an absolute pleasure to ride. He would put his head on his chest and do everything you asked of him.

Unfortunately, he was plagued by problems throughout his career – back, joint, you name it. But he would just keep turning up and getting the job done.

We ran him at Rosehill in the lead-up to the Doncaster and he flew home from last to grab second. I returned to the enclosure with a big smile on my dial thinking: 'The Donny's all over.' But when I took the saddle off him I noticed he was standing in a pool of blood. He had taken a huge chunk out of his heel. My smile disappeared and I thought: 'Oh gee, what have you done to yourself?'

On the Sunday he couldn't walk. Monday they struggled to get him out of the stable. Tuesday he was walking. Wednesday he trotted. By Thursday he cantered and the next day the stewards inspected him. They put him through some light work and declared he was fit to run. The injury scare meant that he drifted alarmingly in the betting market. On race day, when I walked him out of the enclosure he wasn't feeling 100 per cent. But once we got around behind the barriers he had picked himself up and was spot-on. We had drawn badly but he bounced out of the gate and we were up in the front four in no time. Because Sprint By hadn't done much work during the week, I waited and waited – actually letting some horses pass us – until the top of the rise. I trusted myself and I trusted him. I knew if we went even five metres too soon it would have brought us undone. Horses were charging past us. Still we waited. Then, at the furlong post, I asked him for a big effort and he just jumped out of the ground. We reeled them in and he went past the leader about four strides from home. Doncaster's aren't easy to win and Sprint By had done it the hard way.

EREMEIN 2003–2007 (by Timber Country out of Marrego) first came to my attention as a two-year-old when I won on him. He was trained by Allan Denham and owned by Geoff and Beryl White of Invermein Stud in the Hunter Valley. He went on to win the Rosehill Guineas and the Australian Derby in 2005 with jockey Corey Brown aboard. After racing in Brisbane he broke down with some knee problems and was sent to spell.

We were reunited as a partnership when I rode him in an 800-metre barrier trial at Rosehill in the summer of 2005–06. I immediately thought he felt like the real deal and his chances of winning the 2400-metre BMW Stakes at Rosehill that autumn were good. His lead up performances were outstanding, winning the Ranvet Stakes at Rosehill in March on his way to blitzing the field in the BMW in April. By then he was just starting to peak so it was no surprise when he outclassed the field in the Queen Elizabeth Stakes at Randwick.

Although a favourite for the Cox Plate in October, he developed a back problem in his preparation and had to be spelled again. He made a third comeback in autumn 2007 but his recurring back problem injury again wrecked his chances. He was a horse with the ability and talent to win a Melbourne Cup but he was never to have his potential fulfilled.

MAKYBE DIVA 2002–2005 (by Desert King out of Tugela). So much has been said about the mighty mare in other parts of this book, but it would still be remiss of me if she was left out of this section. In the wake of her exploits people are still surprised to learn she was unwanted as a foal. After all, her bloodlines were impeccable. Tugela had been a dual Group 1 winner and was a daughter of Riverman, twice champion sire of France. Her grand-dam's sire, Roberto, was an English Derby winner whose progeny included Melbourne Cup winner At Talaq. Other winners in her family tree included Katsura by Northern Dancer, a five-time champion sire in England and the USA, and mare Noble Fancy by dual champion sire of the United Kingdom and Prix de L'Arc de Triomphe winner Vaguely Noble. The Diva's sire, Desert King, was a son of that sire of champions Danehill. Desert King won the Irish Derby and became known as a sire of outstanding stayers.

Makybe Diva made her racing debut in July 2002 as a three-year-old in a maiden at Benalla, where she finished fourth. The next month she had already turned four when she scored her first provincial win, before heading to the city to beat a field of fillies and mares over 2000 metres at Flemington. Wins in the Werribee Cup and the VRC Queen Elizabeth Stakes in the spring of 2002 made it six victories in a row and suggested she was a stayer on the way up.

The following spring saw the forging of our partnership when she started a 14–1 outsider in the Caulfield Cup to storm home from near last to finish fourth. My impression that it was the perfect Melbourne Cup trial was proven correct. In November 2003 she won the nation's biggest race for the first time. The rest, as they say, is history. But raw statistics cannot account for her courage, her almost obsessive desire to have no horse run past her, nor the bullish personality that she displayed when approaching her awesome best. In 2003 Makybe Diva had won in perfect spring conditions. In 2004 the great war-horse churned through the Flemington mud and driving rain to win her second Cup, beating multiple Irish St Leger winner Vinnie Roe, Caulfield Cup winners Mummify and Elvstroem, European star Mamool and 2002 Melbourne Cup winner Media Puzzle.

At the end of that season, Makybe Diva was named the out-standing long-distance performer and top filly or mare by the World Thoroughbred Racehorse Rankings Conference as well as Australian Champion Racehorse of the Year on the vote of members of the Australian racing media.

On 1 November 2005 she entered the realm of sporting immortality by winning a third Melbourne Cup, carrying 58 kilograms to break her own weight-carrying record for a mare. It was a perfect exit point and again earned her the title of Australian Champion Racehorse of the Year for the second time.

The best horses I wish
I had ridden

The rivalry between jockeys isn't confined to the track. The contest to beat the other hoops to the best rides is equally intense. If sound judgement and luck are on your side, you just might end up on a genuine Group 1 prospect. Then it is up to your ability to ensure that you retain the ride.

I have been blessed throughout my career to be linked with some of the most splendid horses to set foot on a racetrack. Then there are the ones I have had to admire from afar, and often from the rear view as they shot clear to win another great race. These are the gallopers I wish I'd had a crack at riding.

MIGHT AND POWER 1996–2000 (by Zabeel out of Benediction) was trained by that canny horseman Jack Denham and ridden throughout his career by Jim Cassidy, Brian York and John Marshall. If ever there was a horse who lived right up to his name, it was this bloke. He smashed his rivals into the ground. His secret was a high cruising speed which made him one of the fastest stayers I've ever encountered.

When people talk about bold, front-running stayers, Might And Power is the first horse to spring to mind. The way that he took control of a race right from the barrier had to be seen to be believed.

Like Makybe Diva, Might And Power had a great set of lungs and a great heart. In 1997 he was rated the world's best stayer after taking out the Caulfield–Melbourne cups double, leading all the way in both contests in a style that endeared him to racing fans everywhere. The following year he led all the way to win the Cox Plate with another fantastic effort. His raw figures of 15 wins from 33 starts are awesome by any standard. But you had to see this fella throw down the gauntlet to the field race after race and then run them off their legs to realise just what made him so special.

LONHRO 2000–2004 (by Octagonal out of Shadea) simply oozed class and charisma. The name Lonhro is derived from the London and Rhodesian Mining and Land Company (later Lonrho; the 'h' and the 'r' are transposed), run by Roland 'Tiny' Rowland. The new foal was so named because the son of the mighty Octagonal was 'tiny but perfect'. The Australian business world remembers Tiny Rowland as the bloke who went head-to-head with Alan Bond, a contest that resulted in the unravelling of the Perth entrepreneur's financial empire.

As for Lonhro the galloper, in time he grew into a magnificent racing machine. Whenever he stepped into the enclosure, every head would turn in his direction. The John Hawkes–trained colt was as dark as the ace of spades and shone like a brand new Ferrari. He was the total professional – whether behind the barrier, leading from the front or coming from behind, he was never flustered. His regular jockey Darren Beadman told me that Lonhro never put a foot wrong, and his record reflects his perfect ways. He won an amazing 26 times from 35 starts, including 11 Group 1 victories. Fittingly, he retired right at the top of his game leaving us all with wonderful memories of his greatness.

SUNLINE 1998–2002 (by Desert Sun out of Songline) was the magnificent mare that Makybe Diva needed to eclipse to become Australasia's greatest stakes winner. The winner of 13 Group 1 races including two Cox Plates, the bay greeted the judge 32 times from 48 starts for career winnings of $11,351,607. Bred in New Zealand in 1995, she was trained by Trevor McKee and ridden by Greg Childs, Larry Cassidy and Peter Johnson.

Sunline's outstanding characteristic was her sheer will to win. This was evidenced by the fact that we only saw the best of her when she was challenged. She could come out quickly, take control of a race and then beat her rivals by out-running them – they just couldn't keep up. She was that powerful. But every now and then a horse would come along to challenge her. There were times when she looked like being beaten, but she simply refused to be passed. And it must be remembered that she raced in an era of very talented horses like Tie The Knot, Sky Heights and Shogun Lodge.

Her longevity added to her greatness. Sunline was a Group winner as a three-year-old and continued to pick up the big races right throughout her career. That sustained form made her the first horse to be inducted into the Hall of Fame while still racing and a three-time winner of the Australian Champion Racehorse of the Year award.

ROUGH HABIT 1989–1994 (by Roughcast out of Certain Habit) was killing them in Brisbane around the time my career was kicking off on the Gold Coast. As an ambitious young jockey I wanted to ride fast horses, and the John Wheeler–trained New Zealander was as quick as they came. An ugly duckling, he didn't look anything special, but once he walked onto a racetrack he was all business.

He won two Stradbroke Handicaps and three Doomben Cups plus a Queensland Derby. He also picked up major victories in Sydney and Melbourne. Whether over 1400 or 2400 metres, wet or dry tracks, it was all the same to Rough Habit. With Jimmy Cassidy aboard, he captured everybody's imagination with his knack for coming from the rear of the field to weave his way through and pull off unlikely victories. His sectionals were right off the charts.

As an eight-year-old he was just edged out in the 1994 Cox Plate by fellow New Zealander Solvit. But he wasn't finished. The bay gelding returned to Brisbane the following winter to win the PJ O'Shea Stakes in a Cinderella farewell to a fabulous career.

BETTER LOOSEN UP 1987–1993 (by Loosen Up out of Better Fantasy) was foaled in 1985 and found his way into the Colin Hayes stable, from where he won seven Group 1 races including the Japan Cup. He started in 45 races, winning 17, running second in nine, and third in three. But it was his habit of getting up in the last few strides that thrilled racegoers. Everyone who backed him would have their hearts in their mouths, but he would come through time after time.

It's worth remembering that Better Loosen Up raced in a time of exceptional horses including Let's Elope, Vo Rogue,

Super Impose, Kingston Rule and Tawrrific. The race I will always remember is the 1990 Japan Cup. He faced a classy international field that day and in characteristic fashion beat them right on the line. In the 1990–91 season, following a first-up defeat, Better Loosen Up won his next seven races including a phenomenal Cox Plate victory in record time. At the halfway mark he was 30 lengths behind the leaders but produced one of his most scintillating finishes to eclipse a field which included Sydeston, The Phantom, Stylish Century and Horlicks.

You could tick all the boxes: he was a big, impressive athlete with a wonderful finishing sprint; he enjoyed a long career; he was consistently brilliant in Group races; and possessed the sort of courage that refused to admit defeat.

Acknowledgments

I would like to acknowledge the support of Sloane, Tayte and Carter Boss and our extended families; Tony and Chrissie Santic; Bob Stanton; The Fordham Company; publisher Tom Gilliatt and editor Catherine Day at Pan Macmillan; Neil Jameson; and everybody who helped make the journey possible.

Index